Choices

by

Jaya Ishaya

Prologue

————— 🦋 —————

The book *Choices* by Jaya Ishaya is an exceptional work for several reasons, the first one being that it belongs to the rare genre of books that were not written by the author but rather, dictated by a force from a higher plane. You can call this force "Divine Grace" or whatever else you choose to name the direct intervention by the world of the sacred in our daily existence.

The central theme of the work is as the title indicates: "Choices," the faculty that enables the human being to choose between different paths to follow, which is at the same time a great privilege and a huge responsibility.

In each of the different episodes narrated in the work, the characters featured face a situation that will lead them to take an action on which their future depends. The choice is always between descending or ascending. That is, sinking even deeper into materialism or rising to higher levels of spirituality.

Approaching each of the themes with depth and with a literary style that is both clear and defined, the author relates to the reader with great humor, presenting a varied range of events, from The Himalayan Mountains, to the beach, to the interior of a house.

Each chapter portrays the ancient battle between the light and the dark. According to these stories, and just as it happens in daily life, sometimes the longing to raise the consciousness is triumphant; but at other times, because there has been insufficient effort to overcome the density of the negativity's inertia, it fails. However, these are not absolute failures, for the desire for the sacred is inherent to human nature and sooner or later it manifests again.

The teachings transmitted through this work constitute an authentic treasure. Its reading represents a before and an after. I do not believe it is possible to read this book and to remain indifferent.

Choices by Jaya Ishaya is part of the great current of spiritual renovation that, in very different ways, is rising everywhere and is leading to the transformation of humanity by providing, for the first time in history, an authentic planetary consciousness that will allow us to understand our link with everything that exists, and to act accordingly.

We wish and hope that this work reaches the masses.

Antonio Velasco Piña

Author of *Regina* and *Los Siete Rayos*

Choices

by
Jaya Ishaya

Knowing you have a choice
is the first step to making the choice,
and that then opens you up
to living the Truth of who you really are…

The glory of full human realization is beyond the ability of any words to express. There are no limits to the human condition other than those that we artificially impose due to painful past belief in limitation, suffering and loss.

These limits are the lies of the ego: the simple truth as presented by the Holy Spirit is that life is free! Life is joy! Life is unconditioned by time or space or causation: all limits on life are without exception born of illusion.

This is the ultimately simple and true Reality of life. This is the essence of the Teaching of the Bright Path Ishayas' Ascension. This is the Truth that needs no defense.

"Life is meant to be lived in eternal joy and infinite freedom and unconditional love and unbounded awareness. Any other life is utterly missing the point of being born as a human."

M.S.I.

About this book

There is something magical about being willing to step out of the box, allow the impossible to become possible and to discover, perhaps, you are not in charge of your destiny.

We spend so much effort in trying to understand what life is all about, who we are and why we are here.

These were the questions that I struggled with constantly. Life can't be this mundane. Life can't be so negative or so stressful.

People around me were influenced by television and sports... and there didn't seem to be much more. So, what is the purpose of Life? What are we all here for? Who am I?

As these questions spread through my daily existence, I didn't get answers.

In 2001 something happened that changed my life forever, rearranged how I looked at the world, and totally changed how I viewed myself. I learned The Bright Path techniques and entered into an experience of no drama, no stress and complete contentment.

Over the years, teaching thousands of people how to live life differently, I have heard over and over again the same questions: 'Is this possible?' 'Can this be true?' And... 'Can it be this easy?'

This book is to inspire. This book is to realize that we all have a choice, to live life with purpose, meaning, love and joy.

This book is to realize that anyone, if they are willing, can step out of the boring box of ordinary life... and discover how extraordinary life really is.

Dedication

With all my heart and gratitude to the Ishayas of all time for holding unwaveringly to this Truth, for keeping the knowledge of the greatness of humanity alive;

For all teachers of the Truth for being selfless in the task of giving constantly to whoever has the ears and heart to listen:

To my Teacher, your guidance, unconditional love and wisdom are beyond words:

To my husband, my parents and my family;

And to God, the Ascendant, and various other names that mean the same absolute reality of existence.

To you I surrender.

TAT TVAM ASI
You Are That

Choices

———— ❧ ————

Introduction

Most of us experience a 'chaotic-ness', a 'busy-ness', a constant flow of thoughts and impressions that make up who we think we are and define how we react to our world. We live in a busy world surrounded by busy people and fast things. And it's getting faster and faster: we now get impatient if the buttons we press on a computer don't bring up the information we want within fractions of a second.

Even if the world around us slowed down to the quietness of a remote beach, our minds would still run constantly. We think continuously about the future and try to change the past. We are totally disconnected from the silence and beauty of "right now."

The average human thinks at least ninety thousand thoughts a day. That is over one thought per second and is a staggering number. We are constantly thinking, rethinking, analyzing, reanalyzing, working out, planning and reacting. We are bombarded by impressions and information on television and in newspapers that add to this sense of chaos. We form opinions and beliefs not based on fact, but based on what others tell us. Every thought we think creates a reaction in our body. With this continual bombardment of thinking, the body is constantly reacting, mostly in negative ways. This is not new information; it has been well documented for years.

All stress is created by thinking. All disease is created by the mind. Paranoia comes from thinking. Fear comes from thinking. Our greatest addiction is to the mind. If you cannot consciously stop thinking, then your mind controls you. Most people can't. Most people don't even know there is a mind that can be stopped. They believe their thoughts are who they are. The greatest source of misery to humanity is our very own minds. Even in the most luxurious of homes we can feel miserable and lonely. On the most beautiful beaches or mountains someone can be caught up in thinking about something they regretted happening and want to try to change it in their mind.

However, inside every one of us there is a still, silent, open space that goes on forever. A place where time and space have no importance and no existence. A place where fear has no meaning. A place so silent and still, eternal and alive. A place where there is no loneliness because you are connected to everything that ever was and ever will be. A place where joy and peace constantly arise and are experienced. A place that is beyond a "you" and a "me." It's a place so real and so accessible that all we have to do is recognize it.

That place is the true you, the real you.

Your life is supposed to be one of expansion and excitement. The excitement and innocence of a child is the way we are all supposed to experience our daily lives. It doesn't have to be the chaos we continually experience. Most of us come to a point at some stage when we ask the age-old question: *"Surely this isn't all I'm supposed to be doing. Surely there is another reason for all of this. What is my purpose for being here?"* At some point everyone recognizes they have lost the connection to their Truth. They recognize there must be more.

There is a thread of knowledge that has run through the course of time. The knowledge of the ancients. The wisdom of the enlightened. This one common thread weaves throughout all traditions, beliefs and cultures. In some instances it is the very backbone of a people, in other times and places it has been distorted and almost hidden, but always it has been there. Always, there have been mysteries that shroud the esoteric teachings, the inner teachings. Remote monasteries and ancient civilizations have held these teachings in wholeness and purity until we were again ready to experience them.

Amazingly, we live in a time when all the secrets in the ancient wisdoms are being recognized, when the teachings are becoming realized in this world. The original language is being translated and the original message is being retaught. The teachings of indigenous people are being heard, and the common thread is being acknowledged. The incredible thing is this wisdom isn't some hard-to-earn thing that we have to acquire. Instead, it's the most obvious and readily accessible, most natural part of who we are: we have simply overlooked it! But it, in itself, has the power to transform our lives!

Humanity has been trying to find the true reason for why we are here for centuries, yet we have been controlled by the mass consciousness of ego-based power and greed. It has led us to manifest destructive patterns within ourselves and in our world. It has led us to the greatest violence the world has seen, and created the sense of uncertainty and fear that underlies the actions we take. Because of it we protect and hoard our assets. We feel totally separate from each other as we compete for life's rewards. Everything in life pulls us apart, instead of joining us together. But people are starting to see the separation and feel the pain of it. In the presence of experiencing the greatest separation on the planet, people are more and more commonly asking the ageless question, "Why, why am I here?"

Even with this obvious need for peace and harmony for the planet and ourselves, humanity is in a rare position. We have the power of choice. We can continue down the road of destruction or embrace the wisdom as it is revealed to us. We can embrace the reason why we are really here. We can take responsibility for our actions and make the choice for something else, something greater, something extraordinary, and perhaps we can remember who we really are.

Most importantly, we can make the choice to live that greatness. It's not some far off dream, or some hard task. It is our birthright. It's how you should be experiencing your life. It's up to you.

Knowing that choice is here for you is the reason why this book, *Choices*, was written. Most people are totally ignorant of the possibility of something greater. We accept this life as if this is all there is. But that is not true. Knowing you have a choice is the first step to making the choice, and that then opens you up to living the Truth of who you really are.

There are no mistakes,
only choices...

M.S.I.

—————— ——————

Call of the Himalayas

Tears were streaming down her face.

She had no idea why. She didn't understand. It felt as if a wall around her heart had collapsed. Her heart and soul felt raw, with a longing, a remembering. She stood next to a small table, holding a flower. Standing beside her, he seemed not to hear her sniffing. Instead, he continued singing. It was a beautiful song, and a long song, in a language she had never heard.

She had entered the room, nervous with anticipation. For the last two days she had been at this course, one she'd come to only because her friend had told her to come—and when she arrived, her friend wasn't even there! She had spent most of the time looking around the room and out the window. This wasn't her scene. Everyone here looked like they needed something.

She didn't need anything. The teacher was cute though, so she tried flirting with him…but she wasn't sure if it was working. He seemed to give that big beautiful smile to everyone. When she did try to concentrate on what he was saying, her head hurt. She didn't want to know about the nature of thoughts or what her mind was doing. How boring. Where was the exciting stuff?

Now, though, as she stood beside this small table, it was as if all her coolness had crumbled. Everything she usually used to impress people had evaporated as the song progressed. None of that mattered or seemed real. Instead, an ache grew within her. An ache she had experienced before, once before. An ache so strong it had almost changed her life. Almost. Now her tears turned into sobs. She felt shattered, yet really alive.

The singer stopped and quietly bowed his head for a few moments, and then he turned to her. All she could do was think of how ugly she must look, but the tears just kept rolling down her face. Her eyes usually got red and puffy, instantly, when she cried. And she couldn't stop sniffing. He just smiled at her lovingly and handed her some tissues. She dabbed her eyes daintily, then hesitated slightly before loudly blowing her nose.

"What on earth was that?" She asked.

"The song of your soul remembering Home," he gently answered.

They sat and closed their eyes to meditate and her tears continued. She was so emotionally moved she could not concentrate on the new technique he had just given her. Instead her mind flashed on the only other time in her life that she had felt this…

She had gone trekking in Nepal. It was a ten year-old dream, one she'd had ever since she had seen pictures of the highest mountains in the world. She didn't know if it was the ruggedness or the remoteness that had impacted her more, but a seed had been planted. Her desire grew. She read books on the great mountains and on the people who climbed them. She gazed at photos of the enormous landscapes with their remote villages and the people who lived in them. She saw pictures of the religions and ancient beliefs still being lived on those slopes to this day. Years passed, yet she knew she would get there someday. A part of her knew she had to. The dream got put into the background, but it was never forgotten. It couldn't be. The connection was too strong.

Then, one day, she made up her mind to go. It was at a time when most of her friends had already done their hard backpacking travels and were choosing for luxury resorts instead. She was faced with the options of the comfortable, familiar holiday, or making the ten year-old dream come true. She knew this was the time to make her dream come into reality. She had to do this, even though no one else was interested in going with her. Being determined, she planned her trip alone. Once again she picked up her backpack and jumped on a plane, not knowing what to expect, but just the fact she had gone on her own was empowering.

Nepal touched her heart and awakened her soul. She pushed the boundaries of her physical, emotional and mental bodies every day with the different decisions she had to make and the different situations she found herself in. It changed her in ways she could never have imagined.

Street life in Kathmandu was fascinating. It was like stepping back in time. It functioned on its own time and in its own universe. There was barely a thing similar to the country she had just left behind. Everything was new and foreign to her.

The sights were different, with the awe-inspiring mountains, colorfully dressed people, and exotically carved buildings. The smells were strange; with the wood fire smoke everywhere, and the aroma of food and spices cooking. Everywhere were the sounds of bells clanging from temples and from around the necks of cows. Everywhere were the sounds of voices, the hum of life, and the sound of prayer.

Prayer was everywhere. Statues of Shiva and Ganesh were tucked into street corners and blessed as a part of daily life. She walked past doorways that had a lot of noise coming from within. Inside would be a room with a little altar, packed full of people, praying and singing. Incense smoke would be thick and dense, and the room would be lit by candles. Life here was exciting and alive. On the steep steps of the Maju temple in Durbar Square, you could sit for hours and watch the world go by. The scenes merged time into one location. Men dressed in rags and pulling old carts loaded with goods walked past men in business suits.

In one part of the little ancient city, she walked clockwise around the massive structure of Bodanath. It was easily the largest stupa (or temple) in Nepal, if not the world; hundreds of people all chanted and walked with her. This wasn't a special occasion. This was a daily event. The Nepali eyes of Buddha were painted on the four sides of the stupa. They gazed out over the Kathmandu valley in the four directions and symbolized the all-seeing eyes of the Buddha. Slightly below the eyes was what looked like a painted nose. It was the Nepali number one, signifying the Oneness of Life. Thirteen steps led up to the spire of the stupa, representing the thirteen stages on the journey to Nirvana.

She was in awe of the immense spiritual thread woven into everything and every person's daily life here. Down by the river was a series of temples called Pashupatinath, and they again were filled with people, incense and chanting. Along the riverbanks were the cremation ghats, where bodies were burnt and then pushed into the river for the journey to the sacred mother Ganga. Who could ever forget the scene of two feet sticking out of the pile of wood on top of a funeral pyre?

On the other side of the river were more temples. It was a huge complex. Holy men, or siddhas, spent their days meditating there. She wandered through all these sights, fascinated by the way life played out in this country. Everything seemed to have so much meaning. People didn't just go to church on Sunday here. An amazingly fresh and spiritual culture had been suddenly laid at her feet.

She had to pull away from her newfound fascination to refocus on her task. Her main goal was to do a trek. *That is why you came to Nepal, to trek in the Himalayas, wasn't it?* She thought. She wanted to get deep into the mountains she had seen in the books. She wanted to feel the mountains and surround herself in them; this deep spiritual fascination wasn't what she had expected. She knew two main regions were open to the traveler: the east side with the Mt. Everest trek, or the west side with the Annapurna Mountains. She chose the Annapurnas.

Day one of the trek pushed her beyond anything she thought she was capable of doing. She'd guessed the trail would be a gradual incline, but this was not true. This was intense. The elevation in the valley started at 1800 meters above sea level and finished at the top of the mountain at 3000 meters. The trail was almost vertical for hours on end. It doubled back on itself again and again as it would rise up the side of these monster mountains.

For most of the morning of the first day, she was all alone with her determination, but in the afternoon came upon two women resting on a stone wall. She also stopped to get the strength back into her tired body. It was their first day on the trek as well, but they'd had enough. They were on their way back down. This wasn't what they had in mind for a holiday, and they weren't going to go any further. Instead they had decided to go back down and spend a week relaxing by the mountain lake at Pokhara. They were out of here. Tomorrow they would wake up in a nice hotel, a nice bed and spend the rest of their time sunbathing and shopping.

That's what they wanted to do, but she continued on.

For the next hour every step seemed harder to take. She battled with her body and her mind. She entertained the idea of also turning around and enjoying going downwards. She instead forced her tired legs to carry her higher and higher, knowing full well she was not turning around. The little wooden bed in the tiny room she found that evening was like being in a fancy hotel to her aching body. Day one and she was already totally exhausted.

The next morning, she pulled herself from her bed at some insane early morning hour to join the other travelers staying in the little village. There were about thirty people ready to climb another hour's worth up the mountain. Everyone laughed as they climbed in the dark and cold up to the peak. They were just in time. The dawn colors began to ripple and splash across the view of a lifetime.

Thirty travelers from all over the world, and the mountain guides who lived here, watched in silence as the power of Creation displayed It's mastery of color and perfection for all to see. Surrounding the mountain in every direction were the snow-capped peaks of the neighboring giants. Many of them were as high as 8000 meters, and their snow sparkled with the pinks and striking oranges of the morning light. The sacred, pointed, fishtail shaped peaks of Mt. Machhapuchhare, where no mountaineer was allowed to climb, dominated the scene to their right, easily recognized amongst the other mountain peaks.

The people were all silenced and humbled by what they saw. The dawn and the twilight had deep symbolic meanings in this part of the world, for it was the time when the day joins the night, or when the night marries the day. She could sense the reason why these people were so in awe of these mighty mountains and the intelligence that created and continues to maintain them. It was breathtaking. She felt connected and amazed by what she was experiencing.

Over the next week, she trekked every day, deeper and deeper into the heart of the Annapurna region. Behind her was civilization; it was gone. There were no roads, no cars, and no bicycles. Often there wasn't electrical power in the villages. Behind her was her old life, forgotten and gone. Her friends, her job and her other way of living didn't exist. In front of her was her life right now, so full and free. She was fascinated with all that she experienced. Every turn in the trail showed her another amazing view. She saw waterfalls, mini rain-forests, desert areas and huge valleys. Every person she passed showed a joy and a passion for life.

The Nepali people amazed her. Everything had to be carried in. They carried loads of up to 80 pounds on their shoulders. Every plank of wood for construction and every water bottle the trekkers bought had to be carried in either by a person or a donkey. The trail went into the backbone of the mountains and was the backbone of the people. With every day that passed, the villages became more remote and less touristy. More traditional and untouched. Every day, her heart swelled with life, resonating with this nomadic way of being. She was tuning into a lot of things on many levels of being that she had never been aware of before.

She had to walk along a narrow part of a trail, high up above the river, behind a group of locals herding their cattle. She was struck by the familiarity of it, and by the desire to want to communicate with these people. She didn't want this out of curiosity, but because something in her remembered them. Something in her remembered something that she couldn't explain. When she saw the Tibetan writing engraved in a silver bracelet she couldn't stop looking at it. She had the same reaction in a village market when she saw the intricate artwork of spiritual scenes. She couldn't walk away from it. The blue turquoise stone and orange mountain coral wound together around the old ladies' necks brought tears to her eyes. She didn't know why, but she had to have some.

One day she walked into a little stone village. There was a wall built in the middle of the trail, splitting the trail in two. In the wall were old brass barrels inscribed with sacred text and symbols. She had also seen them in Kathmandu. They were prayer wheels. People dragged their fingers along the row of them as they walked by, spinning them and sending the prayers into the heavens. She reached out to lay her fingers on the wheel as she walked past. Her fingers touched the brass and she spun the wheel.

Time stopped. Something happened.

In a flash, she saw eternity.

She had been here before doing this.

Time started again. The experience jolted her as if she had been electrified. She stopped and looked around her. She was wide-eyed. She felt as if worlds had collided within her, but she could not grasp it.

She walked into the village and knew she had been here before. She had the surreal feeling of watching herself watching these parallel lives, happening simultaneously. She looked at the mountains, the valley and the clouds, trying to work out what it was she was feeling, but she got no answers. She walked past a pile of mani stones. The Nepalese had for centuries carved their prayers and blessings onto stone and then placed them in piles as they left or entered villages. They were wishing for safe journeys through the dangerous mountain trails. Over the centuries the piles had gotten large and weathered. Most of them were carved with the Tibetan symbols of *Om Mani Padme Hum*, the sacred chant that could be heard throughout the temples, the country and the world: *"May the jewel of the lotus descend into your heart."* Now, she looked at the mani stones and felt the sadness of a memory she no longer knew.

She walked out of the village and continued along the trail, still shaken. Though other western trekkers walked along the trail also, she didn't want to be with them. She wanted to be with the Nepalese people. Something was happening to her and she wanted to understand what was going on. She wanted to feel the essence of these people and this place.

She got into the village where she would be staying the night at around two in the afternoon. She went to her room and took a shower, knowing afternoon was the only time to wash if she wanted hot water. The water was heated in black tanks perched on the hostel's rooftop and heated by the intense mountain sun. As soon as the sun went behind the mountains, which could be very early in the deep valleys, the air temperatures plummeted and so did the water temperature. She was in the deepest valley in the world. On each side of the gushing river was a mountain that reached 8000 meters up to the heavens.

A few trekkers said hello to her as she walked through the main room in the hostel. The fire was lit, welcoming the weary trekkers in from the chill already starting to settle in the Himalayan valley. She walked out of the hostel and into a narrow alleyway, searching. She wandered aimlessly up the cobblestone walkways. Village life was being acted out in the streets. Young children were playing games. Mothers were with their babies. Ladies were sweeping their front steps. She was searching for something. Something was aching in her heart.

Up on the hill was a temple of some sort. She made her way up the pathways toward it. The villagers watched her walk by. Tourists didn't usually visit many parts of this village. On the steps of the temple, old men and ladies were seated, continuously chanting and moving their fingers over the strands of prayer beads they held. Others walked around and around the prayer wheels in the temple, constantly spinning their prayers to the Gods. Strings of prayer flags fluttered above. Some were faded to almost white from years of being tied to the roof. Others looked colorful and new. All were printed with prayers and symbols. Everything she looked at was steeped in spiritual meaning. In the eyes of their Gods, every action taken by these people was for the good. The spiritual thread and meaning resonated through absolutely everything. Everything was saturated with devotion.

She felt so hollow, so empty and so devoid of reason compared to these people. She had no meaning, whereas their whole life was full of meaning. Her life seemed shallow and pointless. These people hardly had a decent set of clothing to wear; yet they were so happy and so at peace. Everywhere she looked seemed so basic and simple, yet they had more than she did. They had a purpose for life she knew nothing about. She felt like they knew so much and she knew nothing.

She wanted to know. She wanted to feel. She could feel the mountains calling her, but she didn't know how to answer. It was as if a painful veil was between her and "it." Her heart and her soul ached with the desire to remember. She wanted to recognize what it was she was missing. She knew she used to know, sometime, one time. Now she ached as she searched in her mind for what it was she was looking for. She stayed on the steps of the temple watching the people and filling herself with all the sensations. She closed her eyes. The sounds of the chanting soothed her. Soon it was too cold for her to sit there anymore. She got up and began the descent back to the hostel.

She felt empty again. She had nothing to be devoted to.

The next morning, she got up early and packed her things together. It was another day of the clearest blue skies she had ever seen, another day of dramatic mountains upon mountains. She again arrived in the afternoon in the village where she would spend the night. She had reached the northernmost point of her trek. From these mountains was a view of the northern mountains and the wide delta river system that drained from them. She stood at the bluff looking north into the mountains. In the distance forms were moving. She could make out a herd of yaks and the people herding them. Suddenly and silently a man stood beside her, also looking out at the view.

"Three days of walking and you are in China," he said in good English.

"In China…? Oh my God, you mean Tibet!" She exclaimed. "No, it's called China, now," he said with sadness in his voice.

She didn't know what to say to that. They both continued to look at the view for a while, lost in their own thoughts. It was illegal for Westerners to go past this point without a permit. There was a big ugly sign declaring this. She felt drawn to do it anyway. In three days time she could be standing on magical Tibetan soil.

It excited her, but it was impossible. She felt her awareness move out over the mountains, searching for Tibet in her heart.

The yaks and herders had gotten surprisingly near very quickly. She decided to find her way back into the maze of alleyways. Doors opened straight onto the walkways. Behind some doors were houses, whereas others lead into courtyards with little room for the horses and chickens that were in there. Suddenly, loud noises sounded behind her. Men were yelling and animals were bellowing. She turned to see the big yaks being herded right through the village, right down the alleyway she was in!

She quickly ran to a wider part of the alley, ducking into an open doorway to get out of the way of the big beasts. Two other people also sheltered there. They were old ladies from the village and they were shouting and laughing at the commotion. She towered above them. They looked like they had shrunk, they were so small. They were dressed in the bright traditional cloth of the mountain people, and had big pieces of turquoise and coral strung around their necks and hanging from their ears.

They were beautiful. She looked at them with fascination. Their skin was wrinkled and weathered from the high mountain life. The three women stood and laughed together as the animals passed. Then suddenly the Nepali women disappeared back into their homes. She stood alone not knowing what to do.

She didn't want to go back to the hostel, so she wandered along an alleyway in another direction. She soon found herself in front of an old monastery. It had a sign outside saying it was open to visitors. A shaven headed monk approached her and offered to show her around, if she was interested. She agreed.

The monastery was over 500 years old and still held to its original tradition. Nothing had changed in that time, except the occupants. He quietly gestured for her to remove her shoes, and then guided her into their prayer hall. It was lit by hundreds of yak butter candles. On the walls were intricate and elaborate paintings that told the story of how the ancient teaching came to this place and how the Gods defended the great teachers that had brought it. The monk led her to the corner of the room. It was covered from floor to ceiling with shelves full of bundles wrapped in cloth. He bowed his head in prayer, then reached for one bundle and pulled it out.

She watched him, knowing this was pretty special, whatever it was. He unwrapped the cloth and revealed a stack of papers between two pieces of carved wood. He removed the wood to show her the thick pieces of handmade paper. On each paper was beautiful hand-scribed Tibetan writing. She had no idea what it said, but she knew by the way the monk held it that it was of the utmost importance to this monastery and this tradition.

She felt a lump in her throat as she looked at the ancient books. They looked strangely familiar to her. The monk looked piercingly into her eyes and told her that these were the sacred texts of the teaching. The texts had survived at least five hundred years of invasions, retaliations and rebels. The texts were protected by the Gods because they had come from the Gods for the people. It was the purpose of this monastery, and the purpose of the monks in the monastery, to protect these texts for the people who were coming: those who were ready to read the pure words of the Gods. He then carefully wrapped the book back in the cloth and returned it to its place on the shelf. All the time while he was doing that he was chanting a prayer, "to guard against the evil forces."

The monk lead her through other rooms, then up stairs winding around and up onto the roof. Suddenly, they were standing on top of the monastery looking out over the valley. The wind was blowing strongly down it. Behind them were the mighty mountain peaks; before them, somewhere, was Tibet. Her heart cried. Right in front of her, the saffron robes of the monk flapped in the wind. Big golden painted statues symbolizing their tradition were on the roof to his left. The prayer flags flapped eternally in the wind above them. The background was painted with the grays, whites and browns of the desert landscape. The immense size of the delta valley was dwarfed by the soaring mountain slopes that contrasted with the vivid blue of the mountain sky.

Again her universes collided. Once again, time stopped.

Lifetimes overlapped each other. She remembered and knew all, then forgot in the next instant. The feeling was overwhelming. Her soul remembered, her heart cried, and her mind screamed in confusion. Tears slid down her face with sobs primal and gut- wrenching. Everything seemed utterly useless if she couldn't understand.

Embarrassed, she forced the sobs to stop and shyly wiped the tears away, but they insisted on flowing down her face. She looked up at the monk who was calmly standing there, watching her as if nothing abnormal had just happened. He smiled at her, turned and walked back down the stairs. It was as if he had brought her up there solely to have that experience. She stayed there on the rooftop of the ancient monastery in the isolated valley for a while longer, letting the wind whip through her hair and chill the tears on her face. Then she, too, turned and walked back down the stairs.

A week later, she was back in Pokhara, then back in Kathmandu. She had suddenly re-entered the world of time, noise and technology. What had seemed so primitive a month ago was now disturbingly modern to her senses. She had to get on a plane to leave the country, but she knew not all of her was coming back with her. She knew a part of herself was left in the mountains of the Himalaya.

She also knew she had taken something with her, something she'd never expected to encounter. She couldn't relate to her home life of a month ago. Too much had changed in her. Nothing was the same, and she didn't want it to be the same. She didn't want to return to living the way that she had been, but yet she didn't know what else to do. What was it that had happened to her in Nepal? No one could answer that question for her. Slowly but surely the daily life demands took priority and her heart's desire fell unanswered into the background.

But it never left her. Somewhere that memory lay dormant waiting to be focused on again. Waiting to be discovered.

It was six years before she recognized that feeling again. It hit her as powerfully and as violently as a freight train would, but coming so gently from a song. It was as if every string in her heart was being pulled, as if her soul was being exposed raw and put on display for everyone to see.

She stood at the table holding a flower, with tears streaming down her face. Memories of a greater home and a greater existence flooded through her. She felt a pain and a longing for something she didn't know still existed.

Who was this teacher? What was he doing to her?

She realized she had barely paid attention to the words he'd spoken over the last two days. She knew she didn't need the words. The song he sang had awakened something in her, again, that words couldn't touch. She could not let it fade away again. She could not ignore it this time.

This time she had to remember.

Dave and George

"So, are you some sort of teacher?"

Dave sat on the beach looking hard at the middle-aged man's face, a face that could tell a thousand stories. It was weathered, scarred, wrinkled and held the character of his life experiences. His brilliant blue eyes were light and alive. His hair was long, matted and unkempt, tossed into being by the waves he adored. He wore no shirt over his sun-weathered torso; his pair of old, quick-dry boardies hung to his knees. Dangling around his neck were short leather strands with shells and freedom symbols. The man, named George, let out a roar of laughter.

"I've been called many things, kid, but I haven't been called a teacher before!" He laughed again. "Just what is a teacher to you, anyway?"

Dave shrugged. "Someone who lectures you and makes you understand things."

The man laughed again. "No one can learn too much from classes, lectures and books. Those things only help you gather information, but they can't help you *know!*"

"Yeah? That's not what they taught me in school." "Surprising, isn't it!" George chuckled. "But think about it! You really don't know anything about a mango until you've tasted it yourself. You know what I mean? You can read about it, but you don't really know it. You don't know what it smells like. You have no idea what it feels like. You only know what you have read and what you *imagine* it to be like. Words are always that way; they can only give you an *idea* of what something will be like. They don't give you the truth. Only you experiencing it will give you the truth. *Your* truth.

"That's the teacher, kid; your experience of life itself. There is no wrong…or right; only the experience. There is no good experience or bad experience; only the experience. Someone else's words are someone else's experience. That's what this whole world is based on. Yesterday's news. Everyone is walking around with ideas and opinions based on what someone *told* them. Not at all based on what they *know*. They *know* nothing. Why? Because they don't know how to listen. They don't know who they are. Everybody is bombarded with information, ideas and dramas that have nothing to do with who they are and what they want.

"You have to discover that for yourself. That is the teacher.

Me? Well, I'm just a man you met on the beach."

Dave stared at the older man. They had met a week ago. Both men had chosen to stay in little huts on a pristine beach. The solitude of this place was perfect for the growing continual pain that chewed inside Dave's heart. His life in the city threatened his desire to live life fully. His escape to the oceans was to conquer this yearning, empty hole. At least once a year he left the monotony and traveled to the islands. This place was called one of the last pieces of paradise by the surfers who visited it. The area was so pristine it seemed impossible the big hotel groups hadn't snapped it up and opened it to the mass tourism that had taken over many other locations like this. But they hadn't. The surfers that traveled saw many such places destroyed by the tourist dollar, so they treated them as secret. It took a certain type of person to want to stay here, to stay in the isolated, remote conditions; but most of them were focused on one thing, and that was to ride the uncrowded waves. The surfers here lived by the ocean tides and by the direction of the wind. That alone dictated their day. If the conditions weren't any good, there was nothing else to do but wait. If the conditions were good, there was nothing else to do but surf.

Dave's gaze left the older man's face. He looked out into the ocean and watched its continuous power move the waves onto the land. He was much younger than George, but this was a place age didn't dictate a thing. Here, the respect was gained in the water. Their paths had naturally crossed as they both enjoyed the sport they loved, and they'd had many conversations about the ocean, their lives, and about Life itself. They spent the days surfing and sleeping and the evenings relaxing. Their conversations grew and expanded as they became more comfortable with each other. They began to share their background stories about their lives, their passions and their dreams. Dave had finally met someone he could be real with and talked from his heart without feeling threatened.

"You always seem to know more than me," Dave said at last. "You always have some pretty cool things to talk about. How do you know so much about *everything?*"

"By watching the sunset. By listening to the waves come in. By listening to the flow of nature." George looked intently into Dave's eyes. "By watching everything."

Dave didn't like that response. His light, jokingly asked question had suddenly prompted a serious, deep and meaningful answer. "So I have to watch *everything?*" He asked, his voice laced with sarcasm.

"You have to watch more than you know!" George stared out at the ocean, lost in his own silence. "Everywhere you look there seems to be so much pain in people, even if it is cleverly disguised by the smile, the jokes, the career outfit or the big car. Everybody experiences unrest in themselves. For some of us it takes a huge swallowing of pride to admit to ourselves our lives aren't perfect, to admit to ourselves that everything around us we have created doesn't fulfill us. To admit that everything we have made ourselves into doesn't make us feel happy. I mean, *genuinely* happy. Everyone's tendency is to continue looking for something better, to keep changing the outside."

"Yeah, but a lot of those changes don't seem to be that great either. The world is still full of fear and chaos, pollution and violence," Dave interrupted.

"Exactly. When you start observing your life and the lives of others, you see that all the striving for outer happiness is a joke, that it's not a pretty life at all. Our own peace seems susceptible to what the world does. We seem to be totally influenced by what is going on around us. Our judgments on the world around us run deep, and so do the judgments we have on ourselves. Surely life wasn't meant to be lived like this. I mean, hey! Isn't that the reason why you're here? Isn't that the reason why you left the world behind to sit on this isolated beach? People like you and me just don't want to take this false life anymore. We don't want to fit into that silly box everyone else thinks is normal.

"So some people decide to do something different. It might seem like a small thing to you, but it takes a lot of guts for most people to make the first step to move outside of the dictates of society. How many people thought you were mad to leave the job and the security to do what you are doing now? Why? Because you stepped outside of their limited box. It's not a small thing. It's these small changes that make the big changes in the world. The world needs people like you and me."

Dave shook his head. "Come on, man. We are just sitting on a beach. I just needed to get away from everyone. How can that be making a difference?"

"Because we are doing something different! People, in their blindness and ignorance, are destroying everything. They're destroying the planet and putting the blame on each other, all the while continuing to be ignorant of what they are doing. They're not aware of anything else. They are destroying the harmony that has always existed between all things by lacing everything in their lives with competition and the need for solo achievements. Instead of working together in natural harmony, we are slicing everything into little chunks of separation because of our ignorant actions. Our whole lives are viewed and measured on 'accomplishments' and we're destroying ourselves by thinking that's what is important. Or just by plain old thinking."

Dave looked confused. "What do you mean about *thinking*? How can *thinking* destroy everyone and create such negativity? That doesn't make sense."

"This isn't a new thing, you know; it's been around forever. The sages and saints have always talked about this, been talking about it for years, for centuries. The enlightened and the self-realized all recognized the same thing, that "we" are the source of our misery. The source of "we" is the crazy thoughts we think. It's all the same. Once you start to see that, see what's really going on, the desire to experience more of life takes you over. Kind of like an out of control disease."

The old surfer's statement caught Dave off-guard. "Whoa. That's pretty full on, isn't it? That's not cool."

"But it *is!*" George was suddenly filled with excitement, as if his true passion was finally being released. He had been waiting to share his passion with the kid, but until now, it hadn't been the right time. "The idea that there is more to life, more to this mundane existence, is the very key to the search. It is the key to desire a different experience of life. Have you ever asked yourself *'why?'* Have you ever wondered *'what am I really here for?'* Surely the answer is more than our regular day-in-day-out lives. How often are we pissed off by a job? How often do we feel bored or brain-dead? Ever been disillusioned by a relationship? Why do we do that? Why do we think it's okay? Is that what we are supposed to experience? Is that all we're worth? Is that really what we are here for? No. We are not these little victims. There must be more."

The surfer paused and looked out into the rolling waves, and then turned to look at Dave. "And that, my friend, that realization that there must be more, is what feeds the search. The search of the heart. The search of the soul." He leaned over and poked a finger at Dave's chest. "Just like *your* heart is doing right now. Have you overlooked the very reason why you're here? Why you are sitting on the beach with me right now? Or why we are even talking about these things now? Well, it's because you want it." He turned back to the ocean and laughed. "Oh yeah, 'it'. What is 'it?' 'It' is that magical, mystical carrot dangling in front of Man, just out of reach. It can send a person insane, you know; the search is indeed like a disease. It's so crazy. On the one hand, it's the best thing that can happen to a person, for them to wake up out of their miserable lives and to want more. But on the other hand they can look and look and not see what's right in front of their noses."

The young man followed George's gaze out into the waves. "If it's right in front of everybody's noses, then why don't they find it?"

"Because they're dumb and blind." George busted up laughing. He loved talking about this. It amused him so much. When he settled down he continued. "You can't find the forest for the trees. Ever heard that saying and didn't understand it? You didn't know what it meant? Well, I'll tell you what it means: in every moment, everybody has the choice to recognize the Truth. It's like a bright glaring light shining right at them. But everyone chooses to ignore it and to focus on everything else, like the bills, war, stress, the drama."

George stood up and stretched. "Bunch of idiots, these humans," he laughed, "but they're a funny bunch of idiots. I get a real kick out of watching people pretend to be idiots…then, when I get sick of them, I come here."

Dave stood up also, and the two of them began walking slowly along the water's edge. "A little while ago I was reading this book. It was saying how even the great teachings in the Bible have been distorted. It said what is being read now is not what was being taught all those years ago, that it got changed because the guys in power at the time didn't want the people believing in what was being taught. So they changed it, and that's what everyone believes in today. But--"

"Let me tell you something," George interrupted. "That guy spoke a lot of sense two thousand years ago, but almost nobody has a clue as to what he was talking about. Only a very rare few do. And even fewer *experience* what he experienced. The great thing is, all that original information is starting to be revealed again. People are starting to realize there's something missing and are beginning to look for something more within themselves.

"Listen, kid; forget the books and forget someone else's preaching. It's all second-hand information. How many people religiously study the great books...and how many experience what that guy experienced? Not too many, I can tell you. Those people have a head full of ideas, but they still don't have better lives because of it. They are still playing the part of victim and focusing on the stress in their world. Yet the words were written, "you too are capable of this and more."

"It's not some big mystery. It's right in front of your nose, but you fail to see. You fail to choose. You instead make the choices to ignore and to be asleep. It's easier to be asleep. But once you decide to wake up, it's impossible to comfortably go back to sleep."

There was silence.

In George there was peace. In Dave there wasn't.

Instead, he was going over the last words the man had spoken, feeling like he had directed them to him personally. Suddenly, Dave felt like he was being mocked, like his parents used to mock him...and he hated it. He suddenly remembered his teachers laughing at him, and the time when his girlfriend made fun of him. As his mind jumped from scenario to scenario, and he remembered how he had always been made to feel small and belittled, he got angrier and angrier.

George still sat in gentle bliss with his cigarette and beer. Dreamily, he continued watching the clouds change, oblivious to the growing emotions within Dave.

"You know what? This all sounds like crap. I'm sick of listening to it. I'm sick of it. I don't want to hear about it anymore. I'm out of here." Dave turned and walked off down the beach. He was mad at everyone, especially George. How dare this guy bring up all these feelings in him? He was mad at himself. He knew it wasn't about George, but now he had yelled at the only person he had met that talked about the interests he also had. He did the only thing he knew how to do: he went to his little hut and grabbed his board. He was still scowling as he carried it under his arm down the beach to the water's edge and looked out at the waves. The conditions weren't very good; that is why he and George were on the beach talking in the first place. *Even nature is against me*, he thought as he flung himself and his board out into the rough water.

Why was he always fighting the world? Why did it always feel like he was on his own? For years this had been the only thing that brought any true joy to Dave. All the peace and love he craved, he always experienced when he was out in the ocean, riding a wave. Sometimes he would sit out in the endless powerful ocean and feel so much emotion. It would just flood out of him. Sometimes he would yell and laugh out loud for the joy of life, sometimes he would cry because of it. Out here, he felt free. He felt at peace and connected to who he was. Surfing was the only time he felt that. Then he would have to come back into shore and all that freedom would leave him.

Dave paddled beyond the pounding waves and just sat there, balanced on the thin strip of manicured and fiberglassed foam that was his surfboard. He watched the water's movements around him. He didn't feel like trying to catch a wave, he just wanted to release all his pain into the hugeness of the ocean. His mind was blank.

It's so beautiful here, he thought, *it's the only place that means anything to me.* All he saw was nature in all Her power, so pure and raw. So beautiful and beyond human control, beyond man being in the way. Constant eternal power that would never change and didn't care whether he lived or died. The young man shook his head in wonder. This hugeness isn't influenced by anything, but itself. It just carries on watching and waiting.

Dave's stream of thoughts was suddenly jolted.

"Watching!" He said out loud. "That's what George said, wasn't it? He said to watch everything, like how the ocean watches and waits."

He looked around him and felt a gentleness begin to quiet his tortured mind. He didn't need to keep pushing his world away. He knew George was sharing his heart and his opinions with him. Dave felt ashamed for his outburst, and then smiled to himself. George was like this ocean. Detached and free.

George sat on the beach, watching the beginning of the sunset. Very slowly he inhaled from his cigarette and then slowly blew the smoke out with appreciation and pleasure. Dave wandered up to him also glancing at the beautiful sky, a bottle of beer in each hand. Without a word he handed one to George and sat. A grin filled George's face as he took the bottle and flicked the lid off with his cigarette lighter.

"I thought everything was pretty damn perfect before," he grinned at Dave as he raised the bottle to his lips, "but it's more perfect now. How are the clouds?"

"…What clouds?"

"Those big black storm clouds that were around your head an hour or so ago. Hmm, looks like they've gone." George let out a roar of laughter and took another drink from his bottle of beer. "Perfect timing. Nothing beats sitting on a beach, watching the day end with a beer to enjoy it with. Now that is really living, if you ask me."

Dave shook his head in pretend exasperation and opened his bottle. "While I was out in the water, I think I started to understand what we were talking about before. I want to know what you know, George. I want to know more."

There was a long silence. Then George shook his head. "I know nothing, kid, seriously. There's nothing for you to know."

"How can you say that?" Dave shot back. "Everything you talked about makes sense to me!" He laughed. "Well, it *kind* of makes sense." He looked into George's eyes and saw he was laughing.

"Quick-tempered today, aren't we? But that could be a good thing. That could be your determination to *know* more. Passion is a great thing to have; without passion, what are we? Nothing but dead? Passion to know more is good. Maybe we'll talk about these things some other time. We have a lot of time to talk. There is no need to rush…" George turned his sight toward the sea and smiled. "Look at that beautiful sunset. I love sunsets. It's the time when nature paints us a moving picture in the sky, and leaves it there long enough to take your breath away. Just long enough to still our crazy minds in this crazy world. Long enough to bring wonder, peace, joy and love into every man, woman and child, right into their hearts. Isn't that magical? Isn't it stunning? It's the joy of life right there in the sky, blazingly obvious for all to see. Every evening, it's like nature leaps out to grab everyone and to shake them into seeing this wonderful gift. I wonder how many people around the world got to see this. I wonder how many lucky hearts made the choice to see this magic and felt the gentle love grow inside of them."

The men sat in silence and in peace as they watched the colors dance over the clouds and fade into the evening sky. All they could hear were the distant sounds of the ocean. Nature was all around them, dominant in Her glory. George broke the silence, softly.

"Just be still and watch," he almost whispered. "Do nothing else. Don't think, don't search and don't hunt. Just watch and experience."

"Many are called but few see the choice.
You either walk towards God or away from God.
You should not step off the direct path. It isn't always pleasant, but it's what
you have come here for.
That is being willing to do whatever it takes to be free.
There are few in this world that do this.
You are now on a very select path that very few choose to take, and that's by
being willing to do whatever it takes."

Little Mexico

Little Mexico was a popular place to be. Most nights of the week it was necessary to book reservations to get into the restaurant. It was renowned for the relaxed, sophisticated atmosphere. The wait staff knew most of their customers, and if they didn't, they acted as if they did. The walls were painted bright colors. One wall was the bright blue that can be seen everywhere in Mexico. Another wall was painted burnt ocher, a natural earth color that set off the locally made rustic furniture. The tables were slabs of natural wood, edged in wrought iron, and had a beautiful rich red glow to them. Each work of art in the restaurant was an original piece, which intrigued everyone who saw them. Sue, the owner, always got compliments on the look of the place. It was obvious she had loved creating it from her personal tastes.

Seated out on the balcony were a group of seven women. They had moved outside to the smoking balcony after their meal. Three bottles of wine also cluttered their table. Anyone watching these women would have been impressed, and many people did take a second look. They were all beautiful. Even though it was Tuesday night, all of them were immaculately dressed and presented. They sent off an aura of power, a sense of tigresses in their domain. Together, they made other women feel insecure and untidy, made them wish they had worn a sexier dress or more makeup. These women looked great and knew it. It was what held them together, what made them special. It was who they were.

Or so they thought. Slowly, a splinter was starting to fester within their pack. The very thing that held them all together as friends was starting to pull them apart.

Michelle poured herself another glass of wine, talking over the conversation that was getting louder and louder.

"I went to get a neck adjustment from the new place that's just opened up. I can't remember what it was called, maybe a chiropractor or something."

"Oooh, I had heard about *that* place," commented Kelly. "The guy is supposed to be really cute"

"Cute and with great hands," Michelle laughed. "But fascinating, too. He knew so much about what all the pressure points on the body were, and energy points as well. It was fascinating listening to him."

"I don't believe those things work, but I'd love to check him out." Kelly leered as she inhaled from her cigarette. She nodded at the other girls, getting their agreement.

Karen looked at Michelle and commented, "I have been reading about how everything is connected."

"Yeah, I want to get *connected* with this new guy," Kelly bantered again.

All the girls went into fits of giggles, but Karen looked at Kelly in frustration. This always happened. As soon as you tried to talk about anything remotely "spiritual," the group would knock it back, especially Kelly. She would loudly and quickly let the group know such topics didn't interest her, and every time, the other girls would follow suit. Karen was starting to feel frustrated with her so-called friends. Their superficial conversations and attitudes were wearing thin. Maybe all the girls could conquer the world with their looks when they were together, but that wasn't what Karen wanted.

Karen moved closer to Michelle and began to talk quietly. "I want to, sort of, *do* something, or *know* more. Like, do something different. I have been reading a lot about how powerful we all are. You know, like, how powerful the human is, yet we don't know it so we don't act on it."

Michelle was nodding her head in agreement. "You know what I have just been reading about? Life on other planets and UFOs. Like, how can that not be true? So many people see them. There must be different life forms somewhere out there."

Kelly was listening. "Oh man, that's just stupid." Karen and Michelle moved away slightly. Karen took a sip on her wine.

"You know, Michelle, sometimes I feel like I'm going to explode. You seem to be the only one who thinks like me. I just want to *know* more. I want to do more and be more. It feels like there is this big world, this huge life and all these directions. I feel so stale here. I just want to do what I'm supposed to do, you know?"

Michelle nodded. "I know what you mean. I read all these great books, and I know that there is so much more going on than we are aware of. No one knows what is really going on. My brother and I talk about it all the time. We have discussions all the time about the secrets in the governments and aliens and…"

"But what about *you?*" Karen interrupted her.

"What do you mean?"

"Well, don't *you* ever feel you are more than you realize? That you are more than you know?"

Michelle stopped and looked at Karen. "I had never thought of that."

"You hear about these people with these abilities to see stuff, like auras and spirits, with the ability to 'hear' and channel stuff. Why can't we do that? That's what *I'm* interested in." Karen inhaled on her ciggie. "I don't care about the alien stuff. I mean, I'm sure it's all connected somehow, *but what about us?* Why aren't *we* doing great spiritual things?" She picked up her wine glass and stared at it, then back at her group of friends. Suddenly she said, "I'm sick of my job!"

Michelle laughed. "Yeah. Me too. Who isn't?"

"I'm *really* sick of it. Sick of all of it." Karen was still looking at her friends. "I'm sick of all of this, too: this scene. Why do we have to listen to all this shit all the time? It's funny sometimes and I love my friends, and sure, I join in with them most of the time. But there's nothing else. No depth. We've surrounded ourselves with people who don't give a damn… and I do. I want to explore and grow and discover. Do you think those girls give a damn? Only if I told them there were guys and clothes involved!"

"Karen! That's nasty…" exclaimed Michelle, "… it's true though." They both laughed. "So let's do something! Let's get something happening about this! Let's not talk about it and not do anything."

Karen grinned at Michelle. So often they talked about getting things going or doing some class together and it was always Michelle who pulled out at the last minute. In fact, Karen was used to all her friends doing that. If she really wanted to do something, she couldn't rely on anyone else to make it happen; she knew she just had to do it on her own. She had done that all her life, fending for herself. She had a strong determined streak in her. She was so used to doing things on her own, she hurt when she saw her friends doing things together. It was this tug of war that always went on within her, wanting to be in the group, but not trusting them to give her what she really wanted. She hated the idea of being a "group" and moving with her group, but at the same time she wanted them to need her. She needed them to invite her. She needed them to love her. She looked at Michelle, wanting to continue.

"I know! There's a public holiday in two weeks. Let's go away somewhere. Let's go on a spiritual retreat or something."

Kelly moved closer. "What are you guys talking about? The holiday coming up soon? Let's all do something together, just the girls! Wouldn't that be fun? We all could just hang out together and have fun."

Nicky joined them now. "Oh my God! What a great idea! I need to get out of here. I would love for all of us to go somewhere together!"

"I know!" exclaimed Michelle. "I was just looking at flights to a resort place in Mexico and they are so cheap. Why don't we go there? I have been there before and the place is really nice."

"And look at the restaurant we're sitting in," laughed Kelly. "It's called 'Little Mexico.' There you go, Karen. There's your spiritual sign." The other women laughed.

Karen felt her heart sink. Here we go again, she thought. She felt trapped. The girls had all moved over to her and Michelle and were excitedly trying to work out where they should go. Which hotel was best? Where were the best restaurants? Where were the massage studios and beauticians? And of course, where were the good-looking men rumored to be?

Once again, everything was ruined. Karen's idea had flown out the window. Michelle was excitedly talking with the others and agreeing with them. Karen felt herself withdrawing and getting smaller and smaller.

It's like *"them and me,"* she thought, feeling a rush of despair. Isn't there anyone like me? *I'm sure there must be! So how did I end up here? But these are supposed to be my friends!* Karen felt like the part of her that was so excited a few minutes ago was dying. She willed herself back in a flash, like she always did. She put on the "happy" mask and jumped into the conversation, pushing away her growing sense of loss and frustration.

This is all she had. So she had better make do.

*"You aren't here to fix the world.
You're here to love the world."*

M.K.I

———— ————

Mary and the rose

Mary and John had been married for over thirty years and lived a typical working class life. The kids had grown up and been gone from home for a number of years. There was no one to care for, now that her kids didn't seem to need her. She and her husband had been companions for so long that they barely knew what life would be like without each other. So she put all her energy into the cleaning and maintaining of the big family home. That was now her priority, her purpose. She had her garden and her husband to look after. So she kept herself busy. Yet the house suddenly seemed really big and empty. Mary had tried going to women's clubs to fill in the time, but, empty or not, she actually preferred the intimacy of her home. She was comfortable there. It was safe.

It was another ordinary morning, ten o'clock on a crisp spring day. Mary put on the electric jug to make her second cup of coffee. She had been up since seven, just as she was every morning, to cook John the breakfast he liked before he went to work. She enjoyed watching him eat as she idly sipped her coffee. Usually they sat in silence as he ate and read the paper. After she kissed John goodbye, she took her turn to read the morning paper. Then she would have a list of housework things that had to be done: washing the bath towels, washing his work clothes, washing the dishes, and vacuuming. These were things she would find to do so she felt a sense of achievement and purpose.

Mary poured the hot water into the coffee plunger and idly watched the ground beans sit on the surface. A huge sense of sadness welled up inside her. A tug of emptiness gnawed into her heart. Why was she doing this? Surely there must be more to her life than hanging out the laundry day after day.

Her eyes swept along the kitchen shelf. So many pretty things were scattered along it, things from her children's travels to exotic countries. Her eyes rested on the wall covered in photos: years of being together; years of her children's achievements. A tear slid down Mary's cheek. *What about me? Why can't I go to exotic places and have exciting adventures? Why can't I achieve great things? Why doesn't anyone acknowledge me? Why am I just a mother stuck cleaning this house?*

Her eyes slowly moved out the window, to fall on her rose garden. The roses usually brought her so much joy. How could such delicate, romantic perfection not touch someone's heart? Yet today she noticed the dead heads that needed pruning and leaves that looked ratty. Today there was no joy.

A buzzer sounded, indicating the washing machine had finished. There was another household chore for her to do. As Mary stared out the window at her roses, she suddenly felt as if her world was beginning to suffocate her. *Everything* suddenly looked dead. Nothing held any meaning or purpose, nothing looked real. The joy, in any sense, had just been sucked out of her existence.

She looked back at her coffee, then slowly around the room. Suddenly, she experienced hate. There was a loathing for herself and her life. She could aim it at her kids for stealing her life away from her. She could aim it at her husband for not letting her be free. She could blame the town. She could blame everyone. She could even blame the world, the weather, the car and those damn roses for pretending to give her contentment and joy when there was none. She didn't know why, but suddenly there was nothing, nothing in her world right now. There was nobody. She was all alone. She hated herself. She felt powerless, victimized, bound, captured, enslaved, stolen, wasted and lost.

She put her head on her arm and began to sob as she realized she didn't know who she really was.

The sobbing didn't last long. Mary raised her head and looked back at the coffee plunger. The granules were still on the surface. She looked out the window. It was the same view she had looked at from that same chair many times, so many times.

But now, suddenly, it seemed different.

It was so still. It was neither the same nor different. It just was. She stared at one of her roses. So intricate and serene; so perfect and beautiful; so still and silent. Radiating it's own "Purpose in the Puzzle." Mary looked

at it, *really* looked at it. She noticed the colors on the petals melt into perfection, the perfection of the stem. She could even feel the life force of
the plant itself moving into this beauty of Creation…out of the silence…
out of the stillness. She noticed she was barely breathing, that she was
aware of no emotion. No joy, but also no pain. There was no pain.

Mary glanced along the kitchen shelf and noticed she had no reaction
to the items there. She was empty, devoid of all emotion. Curiously, she
noticed there was no sadness there either. Just indifference, clarity, stillness. "Stillness of what?" It was as if time had been sucked from her
universe. She watched herself push the coffee plunger down; it was surreal
and timeless. She watched herself pour a cup of coffee and add a sugar.
It was amusing. She felt distant from herself, as if she watched everything.
Not one question came into her mind. Not one thing needed to be done.
Not one thing needed to be changed.

She looked out the window and slowly a tear slid down her cheek. In that
moment she recognized something so familiar to her—yet, it was something she didn't really understand. So familiar that her heart felt like it was
aching, that it was expanding. So familiar that she felt like she was going to
explode. So familiar, yet whisper thin, like a veil. Like a wisp of smoke, like
a stillness, a silence, a peace. So empty, yet so overwhelmingly full. As full
as the universe and as sacred as life itself. More real than anything.

She was experiencing who she really was.

As she continued to look out into her garden, she whispered to herself,
"What *is* this?" Yet there was no fear, just the wonderment of an innocent
child. She felt connected to each leaf on the plant, to the rays of the sunshine. But still there felt like a veil between her experience and her wanting
to *know* what she was experiencing. She didn't want it to go. She didn't
want her dead life back again. Now was so rich and full, so meaningful. It
was intertwined with joy and beauty that just appeared, as if it was reveal-
ing itself to her. A world full of magic.

A violent ring from the phone ripped through the silence. Mary tried to
ignore it, tried to hold onto what she was experiencing, but the ring ripped
through the room again. She felt the silence slip away. The world she'd
known came back to fill her awareness.

But she knew she was changed forever.

*The greatest addiction
is the addiction to your mind.*

M.K.I.

Sue's adventure begins

Sue's passion for decorating began when she and her husband, Tim, built their house. Up until that point, she didn't appreciate the building skills that went into woodwork, but Tim had been around building trades-men and had seen some interesting and unique ideas. He wanted to build a house that expressed their individuality and creativeness. Their house was going to be styled along ultra-modern and rustic lines, combining the two extremes. They sat and dreamed in the rental house they'd lived in for four years, and always in the dream were all the people who would share their happiness with them when they finished the project. It was a dream they were going to make real.

They bounced ideas around as they casually looked through the house magazines Sue brought home, but the style they wanted hadn't been created yet. That didn't matter. They were both excited about this, and their passion made what could at times seem like a huge, difficult project, rewarding.

They began visiting salvage yards to discover what rustic things were there that would fit into their design: old-fashioned tap handles, old wooden door frames which could be stunningly beautiful if the old paint was removed to reveal what secrets lay beneath, fifty year-old doors with solid stained glass windows. All they needed was someone with a vision, some passion…and the determination to put in the hard work it would take to bring them back to their former glory and join this modern age.

In the middle of winter, Sue followed her husband to an auction. It had been advertised in the local paper, but as far as she could see, nothing they offered interested her at all. She actually wanted to go out for lunch with some girlfriends. The weather had been so wet for the last three weeks that the promise of a fine weekend had been a relief for them all, and besides, her friends had planned this a week ago. But Tim really wanted them to go to the auction together, so Sue decided to go spend some quality time with him.

As they drove toward the industrial area of town, she had no idea what to expect. Tim, however, was in an excited mood He had read a list of the items to be sold and was explaining to her what happened at an auction. The place was a timber mill that had closed down, and the company wanted to get rid of everything. Big machinery, small machinery, piles of timber and so much more. It all had to go. For the next couple of hours they followed a small crowd inside the main building, from item to item.

It was exciting to watch the bidding, and they had a few goes at it. Tim encouraged her to try it, so she bid on some brand new, hand-held shearing clippers, giggling as she made the bid. The auctioneer brought the bidding to its peak, then suddenly pointed at her and yelled, "Sold!" Sue leaped up like a little child in joy. She had won! She grinned at Tim, who looked lovingly at her... then they laughed as they wondered what the hell they were going to do with their new purchase.

Outside, the crowd walked around the mud and puddles and came to item number 108.

"This is it," whispered Tim. The crowd formed so Sue couldn't see what it was. They pushed their way to the front to get a better view. Sue's eyes quickly darted over the whole area and then rested on the item. She frowned. Surely this isn't it! A big chunk of rough, old, weathered gray wood lay in front of them. Half of it was wet and resting in a muddy puddle. It was rough and totally unappealing. But Tim inhaled with delight. When the bidding started he was even more excited. No one in the crowd was interested, so the auctioneer brought the price down and down. Finally, he was about to announce it stale when Tim priced it.

"Going, going...gone!" And it was sold to Tim.

He was pleased with himself. Sue looked dumbfoundedly at him. What had he just done? What was he thinking? As the crowd quickly thinned, moving to the next item, they went forward to inspect their new purchase.

"Just you wait," he grinned at her, "this is your new bathroom vanity."

"What?" She exclaimed in disbelief.

"Trust me," he said lovingly. "Beneath this gray is the most beautiful wood you have ever seen. Have you ever really looked at wood?" She shook her head. He had never expressed this side of himself to her before

"You are looking at a fifty year-old slab of jarrah. You just don't find wood like this in the stores. This is beautiful. We'll take it to the joinery, the furniture makers with an industrial planer, and get them to cut it back and you'll see. It will be a stunning piece. It will reveal its hidden beauty for us to see." Tim stared at his new treasure fondly. "No one else here could see its true potential. All they saw was something too far gone, or they didn't see it at all! No one else recognized it. I can't believe it."

And so it began; Sue and Tim's dream project.

It was another year before Sue got to see the beauty the jarrah held for her, because the piece of wood got stored in their shed. Though the wood got put into the background, the passion increased. Sue's interest grew as they began hunting for many other forgotten treasures. She spent a lot of time with Tim's friends on the work sites, looking at houses being constructed to get ideas. At gatherings with their friends, she preferred to talk to the guys about building projects. Each of them had some interesting story to tell her. Her guy friends were intrigued by what Tim and Sue were starting to do. Her girl friends thought it was too much work and preferred to keep a slight distance when those conversations came up. Other couples were about to build their houses also, though most were going to do it the easy way, called project houses, where you individualize it with a different coat of paint.

Sue and Tim weren't doing that. They were starting from scratch. There was a joke commonly said as the couples shared their house ideas: "If building a house doesn't break up your relationship, then nothing will!" Sue always laughed at that. Nothing could break her and Tim up. They were closer, more together and focused, than they had ever been.

Over the next few months, their project grew and grew. Their ideas went down on paper, and they found a building company. Their shed filled up with various treasures from salvage yards. They worked hard during the week and they scouted the countryside for treasures on the weekend. The only time they took off was for parties with their friends, and there were always parties. Tim and Sue didn't stop. They were trying to do it all and were burning the candle at both ends. They were trying to build their dream and still be partying as freely as so many of their friends. They were well aware of this, but charged on in their dream, which just kept getting busier and busier.

Suddenly, there was more for Sue to decide. What window frames would be best? What doorknobs? What flooring do you want? There were so many decisions; at times it could be overwhelming. What if she made the wrong choice? But every time it seemed to be too much, she would talk to Tim and settle back into seeing the big picture. They didn't disagree on anything; they discussed, analyzed and found a better solution.

Tim came home with more treasures. He had found their proposed floorboards. A storage building over one hundred years old was being demolished and Tim had bought a stack of the old flooring boards. They were grimy, splintered, gray and oily, but he was excited because of their age. "We're putting wood in our house you can't buy in the timber yards," he said. He had found wood that was part of the history of the area, "Wood like you've never seen before." By taking a fraction of a centimeter off the top of the wood, the natural color, grain and patterns would be revealed. He couldn't wait to get it all cleaned up.

That was the task ahead, for them to get the timber cleaned up. Most of it went to the joinery where the workers did it on the industrial machines, but there was other work Tim insisted they could do themselves.

Meanwhile, the days had suddenly moved toward summer. It was a beautiful time of year, with the freshness of spring in the mornings and a taste of the heat of the coming summer throughout the day. The winter and spring storms had passed and people were enjoying spending time outdoors again. Weekends were becoming a hive of activity, as the hibernation of the last few months was coming to an end. Sue was torn between wanting to support him, wanting to be with her friends, and wanting to do the work for the sake of helping build her house. But of course, she said "no" to her friends and "yes" to Tim, and they began to plane the big planks of wood that were going to be their exposed ceiling beams.

This particular day was hot and still. The temperature rose fast and there was no movement in the air to bring relief from the heat. Tim had wanted the two of them to begin working on cleaning up the wood, as the foundations of the house were being laid. It was an exciting time. Everything they had been discussing for the last few months was beginning. The dream that had been paper plans was starting to manifest into physical form. The items they had been collecting were now ready to reveal their true beauty.

They were outside a friend's workshop with the beams of wood set up on wooden trestles. Tim got straight to work. He had gotten Sue to help him lift each of the big beams of wood onto the trestles, and it had been heavy work. He got the extension cords connected with the electric belt sander and began sanding every mark on the wood. Each beam was sixteen feet long and had four sides that needed inspecting and cleaning. Once that was done, together they had to move the beam of wood into the workshop, away from the dust, where Sue was to put a coat of varnish on three sides, while the fourth side would be done at another time when the wood was dry and able to be moved. Then they had to move them to rotate the piles and to make sure that none of the sides got missed, and that none of the planks got overlooked. They had to keep moving them to keep the wood out of their way.

It was heavy work. It was dirty work. Though at first she tried to stay clean, after an hour, Sue didn't care if she was getting the dust from the belt sander on her or not. She was absolutely covered from head to toe in fine dust. They looked at each other and laughed. They were so dirty and getting tired. But they kept going as this was for the two of them, their dream. This was their project. This was for their house. They were a team. They were doing this together.

The day had become hotter, and still there was no wind. They were dirty, tired and only halfway through the job. Suddenly, in the distance, they heard the sound of a ski boat. They both stopped what they were doing and looked at each other, having the same thought. It was their friends playing out on the lake. The weather conditions were perfect for the lake. There was no wind so it was glassy smooth and perfect for water-skiing. Tim had taught Sue to water-ski last summer and she loved it. She would have loved to have been out there today. She would have loved to have been hanging out with her friends. They'd been invited to go water-skiing with them but had declined. Instead, here they were, hot and tired, while their friends were having fun. The same fun they could have been having.

Tim shrugged and went back to the belt sander. Sue went to dust down a plank of wood. She looked at her hands and fingernails. They were a mess.

Suddenly tears came into her eyes as she compared herself to her girl-friends. She bit them back and ignored what she was feeling. She had a job to do. This was for her and Tim. She told herself she wanted to do this. So she continued.

"We all have a gift.
You are here to live your dream, let your dream live you.
Do you have the courage to embrace the dream that gets you, grips you,
or would you let the dream get away and slip through your fingers.
You are supposed to do what you are made to do.
What have you been put on this earth to do?"

———————— ————————

The morning surf

Dave stood in the cold sand watching the surf. The morning sun wasn't up over the land yet, but the light was glistening on the water, catching the top of the waves as they thundered in. The surf was up. The conditions were good. A slight offshore breeze and a mid-low tide made the waves into perfection.

Timing was everything, as any surfer knew. To be able to read the tides and nature meant you knew when to surf and when not to bother. This length of coastline was covered in reef, so the tide had a huge influence on the quality of the waves. The breeze usually picked up by mid-morning and would often swing around and blow onshore as the temperatures rose during the day. Then that breeze would crumble the lips of the waves or even flatten them right out, making surfing harder or impossible.

Dave watched the water to see what the ocean was telling him. He could see the water movement, the rips. They were indicators as to where he should or should not paddle out beyond the waves. He watched the timing of the waves and the sets. He watched the regularity. He also watched the wave as it broke. The amount of foam, the color, the style, when it crumbled, when it collapsed. All of this was nature telling him what was going on out there. It all indicated to him what was hidden just under the surface, beyond the eye. Reading the water was an art.

It also connected Dave to his passion. It connected him to the force and power of the ocean. He bent over and wrapped the Velcro strap around his ankle. He was now tied to his surfboard by the leg rope. He stood and zipped up his short wet suit. Even though he was in the tropics, it was the organs that got cold quickly, so they welcome the warmth created by the wet suit. It also protected Dave from rubbing on the board and getting a rash.

He picked up his prize, his new 6'6" board, and jogged towards the vast ocean. He ran into the shallows and stopped. Again he watched the waves. He watched the white wash, and when the timing was right, he took a deep breath and threw himself onto his board and into a wave. He paddled strongly through it and out into the tumbling water. He gasped as the cold water hit his body and trickled into his wet suit. The first seconds were always jarring as his body temperature dropped and the water trapped in the wet suit began to warm up.

The outward pull of the rip was already drawing him out through the waves. Here was the most strenuous part of this sport. If he read the ocean right, he'd easily move out through and beyond the waves. If the timing was wrong, he'd get caught and worn out in the crashing surf. Dave was focused and easily pushed the nose of the board and himself under the white wash, through the waves and out the back. There, he gracefully straddled his board and balanced as he got his breath back. He was always alert and watchful, as you couldn't take your attention off nature for a second. He felt pumped and alive. He was refreshed from the cool water. His body was active. His senses were heightened as he now played with the power of the water, waiting and watching for the set of big waves to roll in. He was waiting to paddle into, connect with and soar down the face of a thundering six-foot wall of moving energy.

It was all a matter of knowing when to turn at the bottom and play up and down the face, to get speed or to miss the shallow parts on the reef. Half a second hesitation and he could end up crushed on the reefs by the pounding waves, scratched up by the coral, or worse. People had received serious injuries from making the wrong choices, from choosing the wrong wave or turning too early or too late. His focus and the decision making had to be precise.

The thrill was intense.

Yet, Dave never felt he was conquering nature. That was impossible. He knew nature had the power to flick him like an unimportant speck and to crush him, and that created enormous awe in him. Dave respected the ocean. He respected nature and the power that moved through it. When he took a wave, paddled over the lip, jumped to his feet and took the free-fall down the face of the wave, he knew he was totally at the mercy of God. His life was out of his own hands. Every time he hit the bottom of the wave and made the bottom turn, he looked back up at the enormity of the wave towering over him. Even in small swell, Dave still experienced that thrill. He took control of his board, he rode the wave and he was one with everything. With the wave. With his board.

One with nature. One with that force. He was free.

It was an experience beyond anything else; guys often joked it was greater than an orgasm. The girls didn't understand that comment at all.

The wave could last seconds or more, but nothing ever took that feeling away. Never did that excitement die. Never did the awe leave him. The waves could be any size and still that excitement would rush through his whole being. Always that union between man and wave existed. Dave craved that feeling. He lived for it.

But he always felt torn as to *how*. He seemed to live his life split in two. It was as if he wore two different masks. During the week, he would put on the office clothes and drive through the city traffic to ride the waves of the highs and lows within the corporate walls. But instead of feeling the unity of these waves he experienced the struggle and fight for independence. There, you worked against each other. You played to achieve, to better and to win. There was no unity. The thrill was in conquest. The scene, the people, the energy, the talk was all dog-eat-dog.

Dave loved it. It was fast and demanding, with an energy that was into itself. It was as if the heartbeat of the city, the heartbeat of the country, was within those walls. It was *alive*. He loved the constant challenges and took them head on. He felt invincible, powerful, and yet at the mercy of what could happen. But he also yearned for the ocean. There he experienced a different challenge. It was the challenge with nature that produced the kind of energy and excitement beyond words. It was the freedom of his spirit.

Dave felt torn between the two. They didn't seem to merge. They seemed to be at opposite ends of the scale. He knew he couldn't keep running to the ocean to experience that freedom. He knew he was searching and escaping, but he just didn't know how to combine the two.

There must be a way to experience the peace he experienced after a day of surfing without having to give up his career. There must be a way to experience that power and invincibility without having to give up the long surf trips away.

But how can you have it all? He thought. Was it possible, or was it totally dependent on where you lived and what you were doing? What does real peace and happiness look like anyway? We can't all move to the beach. Imagine that. The population of the city all moves to the beach to find some happiness. It just didn't make sense. There must be something else not conditional on where you are and what you are doing. There must be another way to make the experiences he was constantly chasing become permanent.

What could that be?

Today, Dave floated out the back of the crashing waves and became lost in a gentle stream of thought. Many things had happened in his thirty years that kept changing the direction his life was unfolding. One thing was etched into his being. It was the desire to experience life. He didn't want to die old and full of unfinished dreams. He wanted to live.

His grandfather's words had made a huge impression on him. During his last few months on this earth, they'd spent a lot of time together. They'd spoken about many things, but always his grandfather had directed the conversation back to the same point.

"Don't waste time chasing meaningless illusions, son, but soar like the eagles in your own unique way. Do whatever you feel is right for the happiness of others, but especially for the happiness of yourself."

For most of Dave's life, he hadn't spent much time with his grandparents. It only seemed to be something he did when the family got together, to keep the family happy. Then one day that all changed. The family had received the news his grandfather was terminally ill, so naturally Dave stopped by the house to visit. Instead of a sick old man, Dave looked into the same face that glowed with a kind of lightness. They'd sat there in silence; Dave felt uncomfortable. He tried to make conversation about work and the weather, but the old man just sat and silently watched him.

Maybe today wasn't a good day to visit, Dave thought, ready to leave.

But then his grandfather suddenly waved his arm around the room "What does this all mean to you? These nice chairs, this beautiful house to live in. What does it all mean? All my life, I've worked hard and helped to raise a family. Everything was different back then compared to today's world. But you know what? The problems were still the same. You were either happy or you weren't. How simple. Just like today. You're either happy or you aren't."

The old man leaned forward. "Dave, son, make your happiness the number one priority for you. If I could give one gift to you, I would give you that, the ability to experience peace and love all the time. I feel so at ease now, even though I know that I have a very short time left. But the question is, *why* didn't I experience this before? There is no reason why I couldn't. I just chose not to. I didn't need to worry and stress for all those years; it didn't do any good. Instead it made me sick. No one needs to experience that.

"What I see now, son is that it's all just a choice, to live life living, or to live life dying. Do you understand? Why work ourselves to the ground to live? Life should be a joy in every moment, in everything we do.

"I see that courage in you. I see that desire. You want to live this life fully. And you should. Make your happiness the number one priority for you. Live by your heart. Live to love everyone and everything. Live to appreciate the breath that you take. Live to love others and to help them love themselves…but most importantly, son, live to love *you*. Find that love, that peace and that freedom in *you*."

Week after week, Dave visited his grandfather and watched the disease take over his body, but at the same time, he watched the light get brighter in the old man's eyes. The words that came out of his mouth weren't of regret, but he spoke of a peace that he knew and wanted others to know. He said over and over you didn't need to know you were dying to experience that peace. It was only that most people chose not to see it until they were forced to.

Then one day, his grandfather was gone. His death left a hole in Dave's heart, but he remembered his grandfather's words every morning as he got up to go to work, and every evening as he came home, exhausted. He had grown tired of the life he'd mapped out for himself. He wanted to live. He wanted to soar like the eagles. Even though everyone told him not to throw away all he had created for himself, his heart was aching. It was time for him to go.

He planned his trip by himself; he didn't want his friends to go with him this time. He wanted to be alone; he wanted to search into his soul to find what his grandfather had been talking about. So many people searched and searched, but why did so few find that true peace?

Dave was still floating out the back of the waves. He had heard about peace from a few people now. George expressed it…but, well…he seemed pretty eccentric. Dave didn't want to become a wandering hippy to experience peace. He looked back at the shoreline. The long, glistening beach contrasted with the endless green of the tropical palm trees. How small they looked from here. The early morning light gave the trees a blue hue. It was so pretty.

Suddenly, seemingly from out of nowhere, Dave felt the softness of the world envelope him. He looked and looked at the natural beauty around him. He felt love. He became aware of the love that he was feeling, the peace. For the first time, it felt like someone had arranged the universe just for him to appreciate it.

It was magical. There was magic. Everywhere.

Everything was loving, beautiful and still. Dave realized a slight smile was on his lips, and that he felt completely relaxed. It was as if someone had turned a tap and drained all the anxiety from him.

There was nothing to do. There was nothing wrong. There was just perfect peace.

Alone on the beach

Karen sat alone on the beach. She stared angrily out to the ocean, half-watching the waves, and half not. It seemed like she'd constantly been angry for the past few days. She should have trusted her instincts in the restaurant when her friends turned her idea of a holiday around, but she had given in again and now it was all getting too much for her to bear. She couldn't pretend to be enjoying herself anymore, when this is not what she had wanted to do. For the past few days, she and her friends had lazed around the swimming pool at their hotel and pampered themselves, and while *they'd* been having a lot of fun, Karen couldn't see it. All she could see were the judgments she had against her group of friends.

Everything they did now seemed to grate on her nerves. Every conversation seemed to be nothing but gossip—about people they knew, about people they didn't, about people around them. She couldn't believe the stuff that was coming out of their mouths, just how nasty the conversations were. Karen was aware of the constant negativity and falseness that seemed to stream from her group of friends. Everything they did seemed so false and shallow. *Have they always been like this? She thought. Am I only just starting to notice it? Am I like that too?*

Karen didn't want to be like that.

She had become more and more quiet and removed as the girls kept up the stream of chatter, until finally she just had to be on her own. She'd quietly gotten up, slipped out of the pool area and walked down to the beach. Here she was now, scowling at the ocean and the whole world.

This Mexican beach was filled with people; beach vendors walked everywhere trying to lure tourists' pesos from their purses with many different kinds of goods. Karen glared at the sarong sellers, ignoring their repetitive calls and their broken English. She glared at the jewelry sellers, and then the sunglass sellers and the woodcarving sellers with their items she thought were ugly. Couldn't they all see she didn't want to be *bothered?* She noticed people walking by, but she turned her attention away from them. She didn't care about them; she was lost in her misery.

That is, until someone sat down beside her. In surprise she turned to see who would dare to invade her space.

"Hi. I'm Steve," the man said brightly. "Mind if I sit here for a little while? You look so sad to be in such a beautiful place. Nothing should keep you sad for too long in a place like this."

A rush of emotions raced through her. First she was astonished at the man's boldness, then angry at it. She felt annoyed at herself for her thoughts being so publicly displayed, and then angry this stranger dared to address them. All these emotions raced across her face. Then, as she looked at him, ready to fire a cutting remark, she realized she actually *wanted* to talk to someone. She noticed his happy eyes and gentle smile. She looked at him a few moments, and then sighed as her defenses came down.

"I don't know what to say," she finally stammered. "You must be reading my mind."

"It's easy," he smiled at her. "I've been here a few weeks, and just look around you. Most people on holiday are having fun and laughing. You, on the other hand, have been sitting here for a while looking like you are about to cry. Of course, it's the least I can do to see if I can talk to you or make you laugh or something. Honestly, it doesn't take long for all your worries to slide away. It's a bit like hopping in a bath tub and washing the dirt off."

"Why doesn't it all just stay off? Wouldn't that be nice?" She looked out to sea, and went back into her misery. "Why don't they all just go away?"

"The ultimate dream, hey?" "What?"

"Peace. Isn't that what everyone is looking for? Even you with all that sadness on your face."

"I'm not looking for anything," she said, suddenly defensive, and thinking, *Great. Just what I need, a bloody wacko preacher to sit beside me.* How was she going to get rid of him? "I just need everyone to get out of my life, especially my bullshit girlfriends. I'm sick of all the *shit*."

"Wow!" He moved away from her in pretended protectiveness. "So you are on holiday with these friends of yours and they're driving you nuts. So you leave them to go sit on the beach and get some…peace?" Steve laughed gently and looked into the waves.

Karen laughed now.

"Yeah, I guess you're right. Maybe it *is* what everyone is looking for, me included. I had my own idea of what this holiday would look like and it's going down the tube fast!"

"That's because you're giving your peace away."

"I didn't have any to begin with!" Karen declared. Steve shook his head while still smiling at her.

"Most people don't like to hear this, but I'm going to say it anyway: you're not a victim to your world. Your world isn't "causing" you to be unhappy. You are. You're choosing to be unhappy. Your happiness doesn't lie in anything or anyone around you. Your happiness and your peace are always within you. Always. It's your choice to know that and experience that, or not. But most of us choose not to. And so we blame everything around us. We blame our friends, the weather, the room service, and the guy on the beach talking to you." He laughed heartily while Karen looked slightly embarrassed.

"We make ourselves feel better about not taking responsibility for our own peace by blaming others. But what we are really doing is giving our power away. Think about it. We are powerful, peaceful human beings, yet we convince ourselves the weather can take our peace. Or, that our friends can take our peace. No they can't! It's *our* choice. They can't take it. We choose to give it to them, and to sit in all these emotions like sadness, anger, bitterness, depression. Why would we want to do that? It doesn't make sense."

There was a long pause as Steve let Karen see what he was talking about.

"Look around you," he whispered. "Just watch all the people, deliberately making the choice to give it all away."

Karen looked around her, thinking, *is our world really that strange? Were we really pretending to be victims?*

"What do we do about it?" She asked at last.

"I don't know," Steve shrugged. "Everybody does different things. Some people become domineering and pushy. They believe their power is something to force onto others. That then makes them feel better, I suppose. Personally, I do the opposite."

"What's that?"

"I laugh at the world. I love my life and I love people. I love hanging out on the beach, talking to good-looking girls." He laughed at her. "I see people pushing each other around and they seem so unhappy. I watch people getting pushed and shoved around and they seem unhappy also." He paused and looked at her. "I don't know where I fit in, but nothing seems to get to me. I say and do what needs to be said and done, and I do it happily.

"Look at all these people. They're on holiday and they're happy. But, shouldn't every moment be like being on holiday? Shouldn't they be ecstatic about life all the time? No matter whom you're with or where you are? All I know is I don't rely on anyone for my happiness. It all comes from me. Life makes me happy, not a person or a location. Life is my joy. Life should be your joy also."

Karen was staring out into the ocean again. Although what he was saying was right, she felt her defenses go up again. She knew she needed to change things in her life, but she didn't like them being shown so clearly to her.

"In a perfect world, maybe," she said slowly. "But life isn't a holiday. We can't just leave everything to do this. That is why people take these trips. It is to escape. And even you, being here for a long time, people would say you're escaping. I have my responsibilities. I have my work and my commitments. Life is supposed to be hard. I have to work at it to achieve what I want. My life isn't happy." She turned to look at him as she realized what she had just said.

"My life isn't happy," she repeated, more to herself.

"So, what about you?" He returned her stare. "You have just said this holiday isn't working out the way you had planned. There has to be more that goes beyond leaving your work behind and going on holiday. What about you? What about your happiness?"

They both were quiet.

"It's up to you to change, not them," he said.

Karen looked up into Steve's eyes as he stared intently at her. She knew what he said was true, but she didn't like it. She turned away from his gaze and looked up the beach, only to see Michelle coming towards them, waving frantically "Oh man. It's Michelle, one of my friends." She started to stand. "I'd better go."

"Running to the source of your pain?" Steve laughed, and then quickly said, "Great talking to ya. Just keep that smile on your face, and the sadness away."

Karen was already up on her feet. "I...I hope I'll see you again, sometime. Thanks for the chat."

She smiled broadly at him, then turned and walked towards Michelle.

Only full and complete enlightenment
satisfies the life's quest of a soul.
That continues for eternity.
It's a heroic path as there is no end to it.
It's a moment by moment realization
of what you came here to do.

M.K.I.

—————— ——————

Dreams to dust to dreams

Sue looked around the room. Absolutely everything she laid her eyes on held a special story, a story of her involvement. It was their house. It was beautiful, beyond anything she had ever seen.

The wooden floorboards lay in their glory. Their story was over one hundred years old. Tim found them all gray and dirty in a salvage yard and took them to a mill, where the machines cut a very thin slice off the top of each board to reveal its beauty. Sue's story was of watching the guys lay them, of her dream house coming together. She remembered the strong smell of the varnish that went over the top. The first scratch she saw put on them as Tim carelessly dragged the coffee table across the floor. All these memories put the heart and soul into this building.

She looked at the windows in the lounge. Even they held a story of what the house looked like as a raw shell and how it suddenly took form when the glass went in. She and Tim decided the unusual window shapes together, debated the color of the frames, calculated the sizes, and looked at pictures of drapes, blinds and fixtures. The terracotta tiles in the kitchen, the custom bench top, the sink taps; all these held stories, and all were marked by Sue's personal involvement. She remembered how long she spent on her knees using a toothbrush to put sealer on the grout in the kitchen. She remembered how the two of them and some of their male friends stood around drinking beers together, deciding where the island bench in the kitchen should go. They'd had so much fun arguing and bouncing ideas around. Sue had loved those moments so much.

They dug holes for their front fence in the pouring rain and laughed as they got covered in mud. People drove by, wondering what these two luna-tics were doing out in the bad weather. They were continuing with their dream, and even the weather wasn't going to stop them. Together Sue and Tim gritted their teeth, heaved and slid the big heavy strainer posts into the holes on each side of their driveway. Together they got the other posts into the ground, until their rustic farm fence in the middle of suburbia was complete. She'd already bought creepers to cover the chicken wire and the posts. Now the creepers were flowering, with pretty little purple pea-shaped flowers. There were masses of them.

She had proved her value and her worth, time and time again, as she equaled Tim's strength in helping to build the house and finish land-scaping. Sue helped him lift the railway sleepers for the retaining wall in their garden. She helped to lay the hundreds of garden pavers in front of the shed. There was barely a job she said "no" to, and she loved it. She was strong mentally and physically. For Sue, this was part of proving her self-worth as well as her passion. She definitely didn't need a gym. Her body was rock hard from all the heavy work she did. She looked at this enormous project and knew it was "Sue and Tim's." There was no way it belonged to one or the other.

But there was no "Sue and Tim" anymore. This was their last adventure.

Her world had gotten out of control. They had built their dreams the only way they knew how, but now she was watching it all fall down. She watched as their dreams crumbled and fell to dust at an alarming speed that made everything spin around fast; too fast for them to fix. Somehow, in all the busyness of making their dreams real, Sue and Tim had forgotten about each other.

Sue looked out the beautiful wooden French doors, into the courtyard that wasn't yet finished, and stared in silent disbelief. It had all come to an end. It didn't seem real. She would never sit out there, in the courtyard that she had envisioned, entertaining her friends. She was never to see the rock-wall boxed garden she had started to design, or the lovely big pots she'd started collecting with the vision of putting big exotic Yucca plants in them. She would never get to relax with the tranquil sounds of the garden waterfall she had visualized to perfect the courtyard.

She'd had a dream. It was such a beautiful dream. It was such a produc-tive vision. They had almost completed it. Together! What on earth went wrong? Every spare moment was spent on their project. Their passions were intertwined with every room and with every decision. Their friends were intertwined with the jokes and after work beers. It was all so intertwined. How could it end?

Sue and Tim had believed they would never lose sight of the big picture...but slowly the wind began to scatter their intentions and their ideas in different directions. They had submerged every waking moment into their adventure, and suddenly they needed to escape from it. Sometimes they escaped together, but more and more often, they escaped with their own friends. The occasional party they used to go to together now became the needed routine to find their own freedom from all of this constant work. Whether they wanted to admit it or not, they began to run. They ran from the house, from their commitments, from life and from each other, and it had seemed so innocent at the time. There was nothing wrong with it, if everyone was doing it.

Every escape was the same. Every party was the same. The goal was to leave this world and reality behind and escape into a different realm. It was to enter into a place where everything was magical, vivid and loving. Everyone around felt the same. Love and intimacy flowed between them all; it was on everyone's faces. Each party was a place where, for a night, everything was exciting and full of freedom and joy. Even when you knew that, in the morning, the chains of darkness would drag you back to the world of limitations, work and drudgery. Back to this world.

The pill Sue put in her mouth was tiny and tasted bitter, and she quickly swallowed it with a mouthful of the drink she had in her hand. She had felt hyped and alive since they entered the party; her body was already running on anticipation and adrenalin. No matter how tired she was, it always disappeared when they went out. There were crowds of people in every room of the house. The bass beat of the music was vibrating through everything, and by everyone's actions and eyes, everyone was "on" tonight, on the party drugs that were readily available. It was a vicious circle. Every Monday, Sue told herself "no more". Every Friday, people were mentioning where it was all happening that weekend. It didn't matter what age, what background or what job you had in the town. Everybody was after the same thing. They were all there to escape.

Sue felt the first sensations of the drug start to affect her. She loved this moment; you never knew what you had really taken or how strong it was going to be, you were just on for the ride. Some pills were weakened by being mixed and others were potent

It was like playing Russian roulette with your body and your consciousness. She felt the familiar drug-created confidence come on. Ironically, it happened as her body sensations started to numb, and the numbness made her feel invincible. Her brain had begun producing chemical endorphins and everything she looked at made her feel light and happy. She felt love for everything. She licked her lips and flexed her fingers. For some reason it felt good. She was aware of her heart racing and the bass beat thumping inside her. She was hypnotized by the music. Time made no sense and didn't matter anymore. Her body didn't understand tiredness now. She danced and moved, unaffected, for hours.

As the sun rose, sending its message of an approaching new day, a feeling of fear spread throughout the people left at the party. It was time to finish up. It was time to allow the drugs to wear off, to face the comedown. Their chemical bliss was leaving with the fading night. Reality was returning. Most people were unaware of why they were doing this to themselves, as was Sue. They thought it was fun and they did it just because everyone else was doing it. They didn't realize that they were escaping. Sue checked herself in the mirror. Seven hours before, she knew she'd looked great: perfect makeup, hair and nice clothes. Now she laughed at the shocking face that looked back at her. She barely recognized herself. Her skin was sunken in and covered in sweat. Her eyes were wide and her pupils were still huge and black. In her foggy mind, she liked what she looked at.

She'd had a great night, in her head. She'd had a lot of fun, in her mind. She had pushed the boundaries of her body. Now, though, she was ready to go home. Her body was shaking. Her eyes wanted to close. But her drugged mind wouldn't stop. Just that easily, Sue and Tim's flirtation with drugs had begun and their adventure with the house, with *them*, started to crumble.

Their friends admired Sue and Tim's relationship. They thought Sue and Tim were able to do it all. They could build the house from scratch and still go out and have fun, they thought. Sue and Tim thought so, too. But the falsities they lived at night began to overflow into their days. They stopped sharing with each other. They forgot about the love behind their dream. They forgot about their relationship. Somewhere along the way, things got twisted. They began to fall apart. Sue felt numb as she walked across the dining room to pick up her purse. *How can you let it all go?* She thought, as she looked over the room again. Her mind could easily lead her into the pain she had experienced over the last few weeks.

She remembered it, that darkest moment of her soul, when she had sat devastated on the floor of her brand new house, staring blindly out the window. She had heard Tim's words over and over again in her head, but was unable to do anything with them. She remembered how her body shook out of control with shock, just like in the movies. Her hands trembled so badly she could barely pick up her car keys. Her world had spun into chaos. It was a nightmare. It was terrifying. She couldn't think straight. She couldn't move. She just had to get out of the house. She had run to her car in absolute fear and blindly tried to put the key in the ignition, fumbling over and over again. She didn't know where to go but she had to escape from there. It was over. Her world had collapsed. Tim had betrayed her.

Later, when she had nowhere else to go and returned to the house, she had sat on the floor, staring out the window. Her body felt barely alive. The only movement she could make was to inhale cigarette after cigarette. This world was alien to her now. If she'd had any insecurity about abandonment before, this had amplified it. She felt empty and alone and with no reason or worth for being alive. As she sat there, she knew she was dying. Something was dying. She had no will to live. What was life anyway? What was the point? There didn't seem to be any.

There were no feelings and no energy. There was absolutely no reason to be here. There was only a negative, empty hole of dissolution. She had failed. It was all gone. There was nothing left. As she inhaled the cigarette, Sue felt it burn her throat and she welcomed its pain to her body. Hours passed. She barely moved. The world meant nothing to her. People were illusions of pain and mistrust. Even these walls that kept the world out were painful to her.

A thought of suicide moved through her mind. She entertained it. She imagined what it would be like to end it all. What would it be like to just leave? Then she suddenly realized what she was thinking. In that very moment, Sue found the will to live.

"I can't believe I'm thinking this!" She angrily declared to the empty room. "If there is a God, then you must help me. Show me what I'm supposed to *do* now!"

That was enough. She had sunken into the depth of negativity and had found a fire very much alive in her. She had found a raw power within herself, untouched and untainted that was her. Everything else had been stripped from Sue, yet she suddenly knew this wasn't about the situation. It wasn't about revenge or anger. It was about her. She found the raw power inside her to live.

She had the choice. She had the control. She was all that she had and she *would* survive. Not just survive, but Sue would be the biggest she was supposed to be. She had experienced feelings she vowed she would never experience again. Nobody and no thing would ever make her feel that again. She was not a victim to anything.

The powerful awareness unleashed at that moment surprised Sue, and would later surprise everyone who knew her. It was not a power fueled by hate; instead, Sue knew that it was love. She knew without a doubt she had to love and forgive so she would survive. She didn't have to like the situation happening around her, but she recognized her power, her health and her ability to get through this would be based solely on her loving herself and her world. As soon as she recognized that, she felt clarity. She felt a direction for herself and, most importantly, she felt love and peace inside of her. Her friends thought it was denial, that she was suppressing her painful emotions and could be about to have a nervous breakdown. But she knew in her heart it was okay. She knew the pain was now only in her mind. It was the biggest turning point life had to offer her.

The universe had given her a choice. The universe had given her such an obvious choice. She had seen so clearly the two roads she could take. One was of pain and suffering, and one was not. She could take it like a victim and spend months playing the part of "poor me." Or she could see it for what it really was: an amazing opportunity to let the past go and to step into being the amazing, loving, strong human being she really was She walked to the solid wooden door that was the front door of the house. It had been her prize find in an old antique store. It was from Indonesia and carved elaborately like the temple doors there. Though she had total trust in the bigger picture that was allowing her to let go, she still had feelings. She still felt sad. This house, this relationship, this life had been so exciting for her. Now she rested her hand on the doorknob to open it and leave. This was no longer her home. Now she had to deal with selling the house. She and Tim had to close bank accounts, and split their possessions.

She didn't want to do it.

It was like a sharp, two-edged sword: it could be scary or exciting. It was up to her. She had to be gentle and aware of her mind. If she allowed herself to follow the fear, she would be instantly caught viewing the imperfection of it all. She could convince herself of a lot of imperfection. How could everything she believed in suddenly collapse? How was that possible? What was left? What was real? What was she really supposed to do? If she followed those thoughts it would be instantly painful again.

Her other choice was to not see fear, but to fill herself with love instead. And magically, without her trying to force an emotion to happen, she would instantly be aware of just how beautiful her world was, and how lucky she was.

She was amazed by the power she had discovered to experience her universe. She had the power to be the victim or the peaceful, powerful person. She was discovering a power within herself that could never be taken away. The power was hers. The choice was hers. What could have been viewed as the most horrific thing to happen to her was, in fact, the very gift that enabled her to see clearly that it was up to her to love herself, first.

You can become complacent in your life,
but the universe says there is a little more for you to do.
There is no limit.
The only thing that you have to do is choose
and stay one pointed on your desire.
If you do that, you will realise your full potential
and will live a life fulfilling the Will of God.
You just have to take the step.

M.K.I.

——— ———

Forever

She sat crossed-legged on the floor and gazed into her Teacher's eyes. She didn't see a man or a personality. Instead she saw the universe. She saw eternity unfolding out in all directions. She saw the love of God.

How quickly things had changed for her. Some had been little changes and some big, but they had all been leading her here. Even if it didn't make sense at the time, she knew she was being lead to the larger purpose of her life. She continued to let the changes happen. Her relationship ended, her job had ended and her desire to travel had increased; the signs were everywhere, leading her onward.

Then she met her guide. Her Teacher. She had recognized him instantly. She knew he already knew what she was looking for; he knew it and lived it. Whatever had happened to her in Nepal and then once again with an ancient song, was alive in his eyes. This one *knew*. The energy that radiated from him was of the greatest love and peace. The words were of wisdom and guidance. But it was more than that. She had never met him before, yet she knew that she knew him. She knew it without a doubt.

All her life she had believed her strength lay in taking on the world, in being independent and proving she could do it on her own. She was tough, strong and determined. All that meant nothing to her when she looked at her Teacher. She could go on fighting the world or she could ask for his guidance. It was the most humbling act of love and trust she had ever taken.

As a ritual of cleansing the body and the mind, she hadn't spoken or eaten for the last three days. Instead of being vocal, her awareness had turned within, into the still, silent space inside of herself. Her old life, her old concepts, habits, expectations and identifications had all begun to fall away. She had begun the transformation into the real her. Now, the first words to come out of her mouth were of her commitment and her dedication. She knew there was nothing else for her to do.

As she spoke, she melted into the eternity that was in his eyes. Her words resonated at levels beyond her comprehension. She only knew they were ancient, powerful and on a universal scale that vibrated meaning beyond what her ears heard. She knew she had done this before. She was at last lining up with the very reason why she was alive. She had rediscovered her purpose.

She fell into the universe within her Teacher's eyes and became one with it. She spoke from that universe. She knew without a doubt that she had spoken these eternal words to him before. And as he began speaking, everything felt surreal, absolutely timeless. He acknowledged her with the name of who she really was; a name that vibrated with her absolute essence. A name that meant the truth of her being.

Her name was now Almira.

Sue becomes clear

——— 🦋 ———

Sue walked into her restaurant. She had just finished the things she had to do in town and was ready to set up for the evening business.

Thank goodness, she thought as she closed the door behind her and felt the peace and quietness of the empty place. All she was hoping for these days was a little peace and a touch of joy. That's all she wanted. Was that too much to ask for? She sighed as she placed the bundle of things on one of the tables. Today, everything felt like hard work. The lines in the bank frustrated her. The people in the street who wanted to stop and talk to her were taking up her time. She just felt "off." She was so glad to close the restaurant door behind her, to close out the world.

She looked around the restaurant room and felt herself soften. She liked what she had done to the place. Its presence in her life had saved her over these last months. She had thrown all of her time and energy into this project. It was her way of telling the world she was a survivor. She *would* survive. And she had. The restaurant had become more popular throughout the community.

Building the house had driven a gap between her and Tim and pulled their universes apart. They had never spoken about it as it was happening, but then, suddenly, it was obvious and they couldn't go back. It was irreparable and irreversible. Sue had no idea how it had happened. She had no idea who he was anymore. Who was the man she had been living with and building her dream with? They'd been lovers who became friends, who then became work mates and then became strangers. Months had gone by, yet she still felt hollow and fragile.

Sue smiled. The atmosphere she had created here was so nice, even in the daytime without the light of the big candelabras. The decor was a combination of natural and funky. A big mirror in a beaten silver frame dominated one wall, and a dozen colorful pictures of scenes from around the world; framed in thick natural wood, set it off. Native carvings and exotic textiles completed the look. The place felt alive even without a single person in it. The local people loved it. It had quickly become a popular place to eat and to be seen. She was happy she had done it. She had proven to everyone she was strong, determined and courageous.

Ironically, though, now she didn't care for everyone's approval. It didn't matter to her anymore. Even after seeing the admiration for all her strength in everyone else's eyes, Sue still felt hollow. The restaurant had been the fuel that had kept her going, but now it was beginning to lose its appeal. What Sue really wanted was to be happy. She just wanted to feel happiness in her self. She was sick of fighting to prove something. Sue needed to be happy on the inside. She knew that. She knew she felt empty. The restaurant was becoming more of a chore than a creative venture. She knew it was time for the next step.

One of her staff members had quickly become a good friend. She and Mandy often worked late together. After they closed the doors behind the last customer, they'd clean up the restaurant together while having a traditional glass of wine. Lately, with the balmy summer nights being so enjoyable, they would sit out on the balcony together and talk about their lives and their dreams; and sometimes the glass of wine would become a couple of bottles. Sue enjoyed Mandy's company. She was light and fresh and nothing seemed to bother her. Sue felt safe to open her heart to her. She had missed having someone to confide in, and Mandy easily stepped into that role.

To most people who knew Sue, she seemed to be a relatively young woman who had survived a separation from her husband and come out smelling like roses. Yes, she had lost her partner Tim and her house, but she had created a popular business that everyone liked. On the outside she looked good, looked happy and looked successful. On the inside, though, Sue wasn't quite so sure. Being single again after all that time with Tim was a huge adjustment, and there weren't any guidebooks to tell you how to make the transition more comfortable.

A lot of the time she didn't know what she was doing, and a lot of the time she felt like she had no one. It had all been so sudden. Her friends had been friends to both of them, so they'd been confused with the situation also. They didn't want to take sides. They tried to act neutral as if the separation didn't affect them, but it did. Nobody wanted to have a dinner party and have the discomfort of having a separated couple there, so it was easier for Sue to not go. Worse, over the year of building the house, most of the people she had gotten close to were Tim's friends, guys who all shared a passion for constructing homes. Now, suddenly, they were Tim's friends, not hers, and their girlfriends had become distant too. Even if they didn't mean to, she could sense it. Sue took it all in her stride. She didn't expect things to be the same. So much had changed that this was just another angle. Yet she'd also felt alone and insecure.

She realized it was up to her to stand up on her own two feet, and so she had thrown all her energy and time into the restaurant. It was this place that comforted her in her lonely hours, and it was her staff that became her companions. What she would have done without her staff in her life she didn't know. The place was such a success because she had nothing else to do!

But that wasn't enough anymore. Sue wanted to be loved. She wanted a man in her life. She knew that. She wanted to be cuddled and looked after. She didn't want to be alone. These were the things she confided to Mandy over their bottles of wine. The two of them would laugh and cry together. They would share each other's dreams and opinions. Sometimes they went out together after closing the restaurant. The first time they'd gone out had awed Sue. It was a totally different scene as a single person. Places she used to go with Tim were totally different places as a single woman. She didn't know how people did it. Yes, at first it was fresh and exciting. She was having a few drinks and beginning to laugh again. She was having a good time.

Slowly though, she noticed the desperation in the energy. The guys were *looking* at her. At first that had made her feel young and attractive, but then it made her feel naked and invaded. Every conversation that started off in what she perceived as innocence was actually laced with this undercurrent of desire. Even the guys she knew had the same…*hopeful* energy. The first time Sue had noticed it, she'd gotten angry and wanted to leave. Every time she and Mandy went out she seemed to step onto an emotional roller coaster. She wanted the attention, and then she hated the attention. She wanted to get picked up, and then she definitely didn't want to get picked up. She played their game, and then she hated the game. She felt powerful, then victimized. It was so false and desperate. Everyone just wanted to be loved, but they all ended up in these places. So how did people do it? How did they get back on their feet?

Suddenly there was a loud knock on the restaurant door. It yanked Sue back to the present moment.

"We're not open right now," she automatically yelled out, then, "Hang on, though."

Sue got up to unlock the door, but stopped as she recognized who stood outside. She looked up into those beautiful eyes, that beautiful face. Hope flooded through her in a rush, only to be instantly, crushingly replaced by the defense of indifference.

She opened the door and let Tim in.

"I hope I'm not interrupting anything. Can I come in and see you for a moment?" He looked innocently at her, like a child. Sue stepped aside and let him walk in. He had some envelopes in his hand; he put them down beside her handbag on the table. "This is my excuse for coming by. This is mail for you that accidentally got sent to me, but I wanted to see you anyway. Do you mind? Do you have time?"

"It's perfect timing actually," Sue answered, a little flustered but recovering quickly. "My staff will be coming in soon, but there's really nothing for me to do here right now. I was just going to play with some menu ideas."

The more Sue talked, the more comfortable she felt. After all, this was Tim. She didn't have to pretend anything. But she noticed a ton of emotions were flooding through her all the same. Hadn't she moved beyond all that? Could he still cause all these reactions in her? They had both moved on in different directions; what was done was done. He had chosen someone else to be with. It didn't matter.

It was so strange to look at him now. The same face that had been her husband's for so long... and now it meant nothing to her. Seeing him here so suddenly had triggered a heap of emotions, but now there seemed to be a gentle nothingness in her. Just like seeing an old familiar person. Tim looked around, then looked at her and shook his head. "You amaze me. I never knew you to be so amazing."

Sue was surprised by the comment. "What do you mean?" She laughed,

"Everything's been so easy for you."

She looked at him in shocked disbelief. *Easy* for her! Was he frigging *mad*? Was he blind? He had found the new girlfriend to replace her immediately. He still has all their friends to hang out with. Her whole world was ripped from her! All these thoughts raced through her mind, then she tried to reason with herself. Maybe he was talking about something else. Maybe she missed what he was really referring to.

"Easy with what?" She calmly asked as she quickly composed herself.

Tim hesitated then said, "With this great business of yours... listen, can we sit out on the balcony?"

"Sure." Sue said, but she had caught it all. His hesitation. His change in direction with the conversation. His inability to say what he really meant. She had a thousand conflicting thoughts running through her mind again. Why was he here? Why was he lying? What did he mean? Where is his girlfriend? What did he really want to say to her? She wanted to stop thinking, but she couldn't. Her mind was torturing her. It was like an out of control, runaway train. God! All I want is to be happy, she thought to herself as she got her cigarettes, went to the door of the balcony and unlocked it.

"Smoking?" He questioned.

"Yeah. Some things have changed," she grinned at him. When they'd been together, he hadn't liked her smoking. Now she guessed it didn't matter. It was funny though, she felt almost defiant as she lit one in front of him. They sat in silence.

"So, how's things with you?" She asked. Nothing like opening the conversation in the most general way possible. But as soon as she said it, she knew he wasn't there to talk about general, daily things. Sure enough, he tried to make conversation and to talk about daily life for a little while. He told a few stories about his work and about his life. They laughed together and then went into silence again.

"That's great, Tim, it really is," Sue said at last. She gently loved him as a friend would, but held her breath knowing the real reason he was here was about to come. Again he ducked from the subject.

"So; tell me about this place."

Sue looked at him, and then slowly began to tell him about the staff and the new menu. She paused to see if he really wanted to hear all this. The energy was light between them. She let the silence hang and waited for him to speak.

"It's so easy being with you," he said, then smiled at her.

Sue shook her head. "Tim, that's the second time you have used that word this afternoon."

"So, what does that mean?" He defended.

"I don't know. What *does* it mean?" She said, putting the ball back in his court. She looked at him with a no-nonsense stare. She had been through so much with this man, good and bad. It was so weird. Yet at the same time, she felt unbelievably calm, rooted, grounded and strong. Strangely, her strength came from gently loving him, not from protecting herself from him.

And then it all came out, like a bursting dam, a little at first, and then more, with more power and volume. His girlfriend wasn't working out. She didn't understand him. She was too clingy. She was different from him. They had different desires. He thought that he still loved Sue. He couldn't stop thinking about the times they'd shared. He couldn't believe what he had done. He felt messed up. He had ruined his life. He wanted what they had before. He was scared he was never going to find love ever again.

Sue looked calmly at him. She let his words wash over her. There were no feelings of triumph or of pity. There was no sense of loss or gain. It was as if he was talking about someone else.

What was done was done. It was so clear to her. So unbelievably clear. She no longer had to be who she thought she used to be. That was gone. She only had to accept who she was and what everything was. And she had. There was nothing to prove or to fix. There was, in fact, nothing wrong. It had all been perfect for this reason. In watching Tim's pain, Sue realized this to an extent and with a clarity that she had never experienced before.

"All those years we spent together," she began, "I was real. I had fun. We had fun. Life beamed from us. It did. In these last months, Tim, I've tried to prove myself to myself and to everyone else, and it was tough to do. I thought I had to prove that I wasn't going to crumble, that I had ammunition to succeed in this world.

I thought I had to be a fighter and I was. I fought so hard. And it's *tiring*."

Sue laughed. "But this is not me, Tim. All of this isn't me. I don't care about it. All I'm doing is proving my worthiness to everyone else. I don't need to do that any more. When I was with you I thought I knew who I was. I had a purpose and a reason for doing things. But over time I lost that knowingness. I started doing things and being someone I thought I should be. No, it's no one's fault," she said, raising a hand to stop Tim from interrupting, "it just happened.

"It's no wonder we broke up, Tim. Instead of two strong people living and creating together, we lost sight of who we really were. We were suffocating each other. I had no idea who I was or what I really wanted. That's scary! And all these months, I've been trying to find that out. But you know what? That's what all of this has shown me. We had to go our separate ways, Tim.

"And we still do. I can't ignore who I am now. I can't ignore that curiosity. I can't go backwards. I need to live for me. I need to do what I want to do, for *me*. We have to let the past go. All of it. I need to embrace who I am and live for me."

Each word was pronounced slowly and clearly, without the slightest nastiness. It was all simply stated as her truth. She had at last realized what had happened, and saw no blame. There were no winners or losers. It all was meant to be. There was perfection. It had to happen. And it had to happen that way so she wouldn't go back. Sue now saw she was about to leave this all behind.

She was ready to go. She was ready to do what she was supposed to do.

For herself.

This world is made from magic not rocks,
but which world do you choose to live in.

M.S.I.

——————— ———————

One true desire

Mary pushed her shopping trolley around the vegetable department of the supermarket. Her experience in the garden had long since gone, and life had returned to the way it was before, but something had continued to burn inside her. She wanted more but didn't know where to look. In the last two weeks, she'd read all the classified advertisements in the morning paper.

She had looked at new job listings, and at the clubs, hobbies and conferences being advertised, yet nothing seemed to excite her. Her direction seemed muddled by a constant sense of confusion of what she needed to do. What was the right choice? Her house was her life and her husband was her security. She didn't want to change any of that, yet at the same time something needed to change.

She remembered how John had been so confused when she had tried to talk to him about this. He had gotten angry with her when she couldn't explain to him what it was that she wanted. She admitted he didn't know what she was trying to say because she wasn't clear with herself, and later he'd tried to be supportive and encouraging. He had agreed that she needed to do something to stimulate her days and said she spent too much time in the house on her own. Even so, his patience began to get shorter and shorter each time she brought up the subject, and now he just rolled his eyes at her every time he saw her looking at the newspaper. It was as if he didn't believe in her. Mary began to feel helpless and indecisive. She wished she had never mentioned it to him. Instead of feeling like she was moving towards a goal, she felt like a bird trapped in a cage.

Like she was in a prison cell. Like she was all alone.

Mary had almost pushed the trolley out of the supermarket when she saw the community notice board. She paused as she always did to see if anything was happening in her area that interested her, and hoped this time someone was listening to her silent cries for help.

As it happened, someone was pinning a new sign on the board. Mary stopped, curious to see what it was, but still stood far enough away not to draw attention to herself.

The lady pinning up the poster turned to her and smiled. She continued to look at Mary with a genuine warmth and love. The eyes that locked onto hers were filled with laughter and peace. Mary grew embarrassed. She looked down quickly, then up at the notice board, pretending to be interested in one of the other articles. The lady stepped aside, yet continued to stand there. Mary continued to pretend to read, but finally, curiosity got the better of her and she looked at the article the lady had just put up. Her heart suddenly expanded as she read the words. She felt the excitement and the hope rise in her. She turned to the woman.

"Are you teaching this workshop on meditation?" She asked. "Yes."

Mary's excitement grew. "I'd love to go. It sounds wonderful. I think it's what I need, but…" Her voice suddenly trailed off. There was a pause as she tried to fight the demons in her mind. Though she was genuinely interested in what the poster had to offer, suddenly there was a bombardment of negative thoughts telling her not to do it. She feared getting dragged into something she didn't really want to do. Suddenly, Mary could think of a hundred reasons not to go, that her life was okay. That she really needed to be home all the time to answer the phone for her husband and even to walk the dog. She looked around as if trying to escape. She didn't want to feel like she had to commit to anything. The lady simply smiled and gave her a business sized card.

"That's all right. Just think about it. I have trust that you'll do what's best. You just need to follow your heart. Have trust in yourself."

"I'm just a housewife," Mary said, trying to justify her lack of trust to this stranger. "I just need to see what my husband thinks." It was a silly little lie, an excuse to get out of this situation. But as soon as the words were out of her mouth, Mary felt angry with herself for saying them. Did she really need to wait to see what John said? Was she really that dependent on him? He'd teased her for not being able to stand on her own two feet. He wanted her to make up her own mind. But could she?

"I...I don't know why I said that," Mary stammered, suddenly feeling hopeless.

"That's okay," the lady smiled, "you just need to let go of who you think you are and step into who you really are. And sometimes that takes a lot of courage. That's why I teach this, to gently guide people to discover who they really are. It's a beautiful adventure once we have the courage to begin."

Mary sighed. She felt so much trust towards this stranger. Here was someone who really was listening to her, someone who wanted to talk to her about where she was at. Here, finally, was someone who wasn't impatient with her, or treating her like she should know better. Mary felt relaxed and comfortable in this woman's presence.

The lady pointed to the sign. "All the information is on this poster, and some more is on the card I just gave you. If you have any questions, just give me a call. I'll be very happy to answer them." She bent to pick up her bag and was about to go.

"I have a question right now!" Mary said, startled at her own outburst. The lady stopped and looked at her, and Mary just shrugged. She didn't know what she was going to say.

There was silence. The lady just waited for her. Mary took a deep breath.

"I used to have so many desires. Or maybe they were fantasies. I'm not too sure. But I used to think about them a lot. Like what if I had a different life or what would it be like to be rich and traveling everywhere." She looked at the lady, slightly embarrassed. They both laughed together. "But then something happened," she continued. "And lately, I seem to only have one desire. But I don't really know what it is. I just seem to be looking and looking for the answer to my question, and I don't know what my question is, and I don't know what I'm looking for. Does that make any sense?" She looked at the lady, who nodded as Mary continued.

"Sometimes there seems to be no desire. And that is even more painful. In fact it's all painful and just so confusing. Sometimes I feel passionate and excited, and other times I feel no passion; in fact I just want to give up. I know I want to do something," she gestured to the notice board, "but I don't want to do something and feel let down if it's not what I've been looking for…whatever that is." She laughed. "I can't believe I'm telling you all of this. It makes no sense to me."

"It makes sense to me," the lady simply said. She smiled gently and lovingly at Mary. "There are two types of desires." She spoke softly and slowly, with all her attention on Mary. "One comes from your head and one comes from your heart. The desires that come from your head are the ones that dominate most people's reality. That is because these desires voice themselves loudly and seem to make a lot of sense. These desires could be about our own assets or about other people, but always they are based in seeing lack and needing something from others or the world. These desires are based in the idea that something out there is going to give us our happiness. So we bounce around in the world of those desires hoping to make a better life for ourselves. We jump from idea to idea, from desire to desire, from object to object, and it's a never-ending list. It's very painful, as we never feel complete. We might feel a sense of being complete for a while, but then we want something else or something to change. Then we feel the incompleteness again.

"The other desire is the desire of the heart. It's the natural movement of the Holy Spirit. Or if you don't like that word, it's a natural movement of consciousness. The natural desire of the heart is to know who it is. To experience who it really is; the experience of endless love, continual peace and the source of creation. To know that everything else is also that source and for all to recognize and merge into One. That's the whole reason why we are on this planet, to realize that. Everything that has happened to you and every decision you've made has been following that one true desire of the heart to wake up and know itself more."

Mary looked surprised, then suspicious. "Everything?"

The woman grinned and nodded. "Even if you haven't been aware of it, that is what has been happening. There hasn't been a single mistake made in your life. Everything has been for you to recognize the greatness of who you are, whether you are aware of it or not.

"The heart desire is our natural desire, our true desire. It's the ultimate desire underlying all other desires. That is how consciousness evolves and expands. Through us. Through the human nervous system and through the human becoming more and more aware. By us moving into higher states of consciousness. That's how important you are. We think we are here living these little unimportant lives, with the jobs and the bills and our little problems. But what we are really doing is huge. By recognizing who we really are and dissolving into that, we are expanding consciousness and healing the planet. Us knowing and living the truth allows others to move into that vibration and into that awareness. We then become the examples for others that the dream of our heart is real. That life can be lived in unconditional love permanently. Other people recognize that, and then they recognize their own true desire also. And so consciousness continues to expand more."

Mary nodded as this all made sense to her. Her most intimate thoughts were perfectly normal. But how did this lady know so much? She continued to listen.

"The most beautiful thing is knowing, really knowing, that everything we have done has been perfect for moving us to want more. To recognize in ourselves there is more, a greater experience…and then to choose for that. Nothing we have done is wrong. Nothing was a mistake. It was all part of our evolution, moving us toward recognizing the ultimate goal. In fact, as you start to recognize this reality more and more, the whole idea of it being a 'goal' seems ridiculous. Instead it becomes recognized as being our natural state. It's our natural way of being. It's the natural way to live. Everything else is seen as being totally unnatural.

"We live with a lot of fear in this world and we believe that it's just a normal part of life, but it's so not a normal part of who we are. The truth is, fear is recognized as a creation from our mind, from our unconscious habits, and it's not necessary. Life is, instead, this amazing playground of consciousness expressing itself. That's what the Kingdom of Heaven is. Hell is the negative creations in our mind. Heaven is our natural state. It's not some religious belief. It's a real living experience, right here, right now. We just don't recognize it. So we spend our lives ignoring the greatest experience that can be ours to be lived. It's like looking at a beautiful diamond, right now, and experiencing all the joy and love the diamond brings to us…but we start to think about tomorrow, and the things we have to do, and the things we should have said yesterday. We think about the problems we are having with certain people. We totally forget about the diamond as we focus on those thoughts. Days and weeks might go by, and then years. We doubt if the diamond ever existed because the thoughts seem more real. Even if we do remember the diamond, we might find the thoughts more appealing to think about than finding the diamond again.

"But the funny thing is that the diamond is still there. It never went anywhere. We've just chosen not to look at it." The lady paused, then laughed slightly. "And that's what has happened to most of the people on the planet. They've just failed to experience the greatest thing available to them, the very thing that will bring them peace and love and joy beyond their imagination. The truth of who they are."

Mary didn't know what to say. Both of the ladies were silent for a few moments.

"I hope I didn't overload you with information."

"No, of course you didn't," Mary answered. "It's just that this is the first time I've ever heard about my reason for being here. I have sometimes wondered, and lately I have been wondering more. I was wondering if I had wasted my life, spending it on my family and not on me. What you have just said is amazing, and I know it's true." She smiled. "I feel so great."

They both laughed together. Mary felt so expanded. She felt so in love with her life. The woman nodded.

"So, if you have anything you want to ask me about, just call me." With that she picked up her things and began to walk away, then stopped and looked back at Mary.

"Maybe I will see you at the workshop." She winked, laughed and walked off.

Joy bubbled inside of Mary. Something had just fallen into her lap. She had just met the person she had been praying for. She looked at the sign the woman had pinned to the notice board only minutes before. It now seemed like an eternity ago. Her whole life had changed. She read the words again: "Change your life by changing yourself. Discover the joy of living again."

It felt like the words were seeping in through the pores of Mary's skin. She felt like she had inhaled the magic in the words and in the universe. She knew it was real. She knew it with all her heart.

"Just pretend this is the only moment that exists."
Manyu Ishaya

———— ————

The bigger picture

Karen heard the girls walk noisily into their hotel suite. By the sounds, they'd bought a lot of things and were very excited about it. Kelly strolled into their room. She looked great. But then, all she had done for the past five days was sunbathe by the hotel's beautiful big pool. Her tropical tan was heightened by her bright yellow halter-top and white Capri pants.

"So what have you been doing since we've been out?" She demanded. Kelly had a way of making you feel defensive as soon as she directed attention at you.

"I've been writing," Karen casually replied.

"Writing what?"

"Oh, just some stuff. I met up with that guy Steve again while you were all out and I'm feeling so relaxed."

"You're not seeing him, like, *seeing* him are you?" Kelly gave her a look of disgust, making clear what she thought of Steve.

"No." Karen sighed at her friend's lack of grace. "It's not like that at all. It's just that, it's nice to hang out with someone who thinks like I do. Like, exactly like I do. He's like this interesting person who was sent to put me back on track, to see some reality in this place." All the girls had now walked into the room and had caught that part of the conversation.

"What? I swear, Karen, I don't get you. The only thing off-track I see is you're spending so much time on your own," Rebecca said irritably.

"Yeah. This was supposed to be the girls' time out, and you keep going off on your own," Kelly said. "You've gone all weird on us."

"You didn't have to come, you know, if you really didn't want to," Ali joined in.

"Why don't you just snap out of it and have some fun with us?" Kelly finished. "All this deep and meaningful stuff is okay if that's what you want, but you're isolating yourself from everything. That can't be too good for your spiritual whatever."

Karen felt like she was being attacked. *They always think the opposite to what I want*, she thought. Why couldn't they just leave her alone?

"Come on, girls," she laughed to lighten everything up—and to move their attention away from her. "I just wanted to stay here and have some quiet time while you all wanted to shop, and you sound like you had fun. I personally don't see anything wrong. I'm just doing what I want to do. Sounds like a great holiday to me!"

"Yeah, it's great." All the sarcasm in the world came out of Kelly's mouth. "I think you must be going through some sort of phase. We're your friends. We know you. But that's okay. You just do what you want to do. We'll keep a glass of wine on the table for you anytime." Kelly walked out of the room. "Speaking of which: glass anyone? We just bought a few bottles of this fantastic wine, Karen. It's our last day here at the beach, and almost the end of our holiday, you know, so it must be wine time. Come and have some fun with us."

The others followed Kelly out of the room; they had already forgotten Karen. Their attention was on partying, again. Michelle stayed in the room. She sat down on the bed.

"So, what are you writing?" she asked.

"Oh, I'll read it to you some other time. I'm not in the mood now. The other girls have a knack for deflating that. How was the shopping?"

"The same. Same shops, same clothes, same people. I got some cute shoes though."

"That's nice," Karen said absentmindedly. The two girls looked at each other.

"I've been thinking," said Karen, stretching out on the bed. Michelle smiled and sat comfortably on the bed with her, leaning against the wall. "I wanted to go away on this trip so it could change me. I had a complete idea of how it would look. Isn't that funny? I imagined a retreat with silence, waterfalls, tropical gardens, yoga and massage…" both of them laughed. "But instead, I'm here. In a hotel with all us girls, still partying, still shopping, and still talking crap. Exactly the same things we do at home. Nothing has changed except the environment we are drinking in." Karen shook her head, then suddenly looked at Michelle and smiled. "Michelle, I thought I had to go to a spiritual 'place' to find who I really am. But you know what? I think I found it here!"

"What do you mean?" Michelle was intrigued. "Here? In this room?"

Karen was a bit surprised by her friend's lack of understanding. "Well, um, yes and no. It's not about the location. Oh, I'm sure a nice location would make me feel good. But that's not the answer, because I'd go home and the good feeling would fade away, as it always does. Every holiday I go on is like that.

"No, it's not about the location at all. It's about me! I feel like I just woke up to something, but at the same time I don't know what. Like, it's exciting--but not exciting--all at the same time. It's like it's right at the tip of my fingertips but just out of reach because I can't quite grasp it. All I know is I don't want to go backwards. I don't want to go back home and lose this. I don't want to forget. I don't want to make unconscious choices anymore."

"What is it you don't want to forget, if you don't know what it is?" Michelle asked.

Karen paused. She knew the words weren't making any sense. She was trying to tell the only person she thought would understand the sensations she was experiencing.

"Something has happened, Michelle. That's all I can say. Everything just seems to feel different. I've only met up with Steve a few times, but he has been showing me things that make so much sense, and they're not crazy things. They're about the way everyone lives, yet misses the greatness of their life. It feels like something is about to happen to me, for me. Like I've outgrown my old boots and can't go back and try to put them back on. They're finished, but the new boots aren't yet on my feet. I don't want to lose this, whatever it is. I'm scared and excited, because so much is changing."

Michelle stared. "Karen, you are scaring me. You haven't changed. Like the others said, you're the same person. We know you. We know who you are, and you're the same. To me you are, anyway."

The two girlfriends looked at each other. One, trying to grasp what her friend was going through. The other looking at her last hope, realizing even her closest friend didn't understand, or didn't want to understand what she'd been trying to tell her. Karen looked at Michelle, knowing everything was going to change. She knew she couldn't compromise her own desire much longer. No matter how much she loved her friends, she was going to have to follow her heart. She stood up.

"Well, hadn't we better go and join the others? I have to get back in their good books don't I?"

They laughed and walked out into the main room of the hotel suite. The girls were all there. The wine had already been opened and two glasses were poured and waiting for them.

"We knew you would join us eventually," Kelly joked. She was walking around in her skimpy underwear. "Let's get our bikinis on and go down to the pool. It's our last day, Karen. We want you to have some fun with us."

On the pool deck, they found chairs available in the section that still had the afternoon sun on it. All Karen's girlfriends seemed to take a long time to get themselves comfortable. They had bikinis to rearrange, towels to lie on. Karen simply sat down and watched the people around her. From behind her sunglasses, she could observe all the interactions going on. All the games people were playing. She could hear Steve's words from earlier that day.

"It all just seems like a play, a comical play. We're all just acting out our parts, all pretending to be these personalities with these lives and dramas. But something greater exists, something that holds it all in place. It holds it all in balance, and that allows for all the movement to occur. All these lessons look like they are being learned, when in reality there is no lesson. How can there be, from the infinite wisdom of the creator? The energy, the force that holds all, embraces all and also creates and destroys all. That is the natural movement of all things. Everything comes and goes except that force. That force is forever, eternally there. It's alive, powerful, loving and real.

"That force is also you. You are the creator of all. That's really and truly who the human is, yet the human identifies with less, and so lives less, acts out less, knows less and experiences less. Identify with the force instead, Karen. Know that. Experience that and see the truth of who you are."

Karen looked around the pool area, trying to see the force. She thought about it for a while. She noticed Kelly looking at her.

"Why are you frowning?"

"Oh, no reason. I was just trying to see who was over there," Karen lied.

"Oh, those girls," Kelly smirked. "They're no competition, if that's what you're thinking. We're much better than them!"

Karen's jaw dropped in surprise. She'd never realized how nasty and false her friends sounded before. Had they always been like this? Had she been like this also?

She closed her eyes, pretending to sunbathe, but in reality she was shutting them all out. *What am I doing here?* Was all she could think over and over in her mind.

The next day, they were in the city. Not just any city, but the biggest city in the world: Mexico City. Karen was glad they had decided to spend a day here before they flew home. The beach could have been any beach in the world, but Mexico City was something else. It was history, culture and an energy she hadn't experienced before. It wasn't a negative energy like other cities seemed to have; well, Karen didn't think so. It was alive. It was as if she could feel the heart beat of the country within the historic buildings and in the pavement. She could sense an awakening of a powerful energy in the faces of the people on the street.

The group of girlfriends were in two taxis, headed for the Zocalo, or city center. Karen was silent and fascinated as she looked out the window. They passed by many beautiful parks and trees. The month was April and the city was painted a soft purple. For a few weeks of the year the natural beauty from the jacaranda blossoms reached high into the skyline and fell to the footpaths and roadsides. It was stunning.

They took the taxis to the huge center of the city and got out at the massive marble building of the Palacio de Bellas Artes. The whole structure was slowly sinking into the old lake bed; in fact, most of Mexico's historic center was sinking. It had all been built on a filled in lake. The building itself was beautiful, however. It was grand and had an air of class and wealth.

The girls decided to walk the eight blocks to the Zocalo. All the buildings along the street were extremely old. Elaborate sculptures and antique tiles adorned the facades. Kelly wanted to go into a clothing store on the left side of the street, but Michelle noticed an old stone archway on the right. She was overcome with curiosity and tugged at Karen's arm.

The two left the group to see what was behind the archway, since there were no signs to let people know. The archway opened up into a big stone courtyard. It was deserted except for a few people standing around a doorway at the far side. The wall the door was set into was plain, but the door was massive, it was easily fifteen feet tall. What on earth could be behind such a plain, nondescript wall? The girls looked at each other, then silently agreed to find out together. They quickly crossed the courtyard and approached the massive doors.

As they entered the building an enormous silence and sense of awe took over. The room they entered into had high, vaulted ceilings soaring to over thirty feet. The wall in front of them was covered by a massive painting of the Virgin Mother of Mexico. It was the picture of the woman who could be seen all over the country, the beloved Guadalupe. As they silently turned to their right, there was an open room that ended at the wall: it was a shrine. The whole shrine was covered with statues of priests and great saints. In the center again was Guadalupe. At least ten people were kneeling on the seats and stools provided, in prayer to the Holy Mother of Mothers.

Both Michelle and Karen felt silenced by the room, by the worship and the energy as thick as cloth.

To their left was another opening, into another room. They slowly and silently went through. The passageway opened up into the heart of the cathedral. To both their left and right was an enormous room, with soaring thirty-foot pillars reaching to the arched ceiling and massive paintings of the days of Christ and other great teachers. They couldn't help but feel the presence of the Divine. The energy was of love, so much love. This wasn't a church to repent the sins of the mortal sinner. It was a place of recognizing the love of the creator in the female aspect. The people that walked by were enlivened by this place.

At the far end of the room was the main alter, which covered the whole wall and ceiling. It was massive, adorned with sculptures of angels, holy men, and in the center was a statue of Mary, The Mother of All, protecting her children and loving them all eternally and unconditionally. Both Michelle and Karen slowly walked up to the front. They looked at each other wide-eyed with the experience of Divinity. Karen felt caressed and enveloped by the Presence. Tears welled up in her eyes for the beauty so often ignored, for life and for love.

As they walked out Michelle turned to Karen. "You know, I'm not a religious person, but that was the most beautiful experience I have ever had. That place was amazing." Karen agreed. Words didn't come close to the experience of the devotional love for life itself. They both were silenced as they returned to the store where their girlfriends still were.

They entered into a store with loud rock music, bright track lighting and funky clothes. It was so harsh and jolting compared to the surreal nature of the last fifteen minutes. The moment of reverence dissolved and Karen knew there was nothing she could share with her friends about experiencing that sacred space she had stumbled upon. She looked at her friends and the surroundings, again feeling removed from the shallowness she saw everywhere.

They walked the next six blocks past the endless gold markets. Suddenly the mass of people on the street opened up into the most enormous square. It was flanked on three sides by huge impressive buildings, and on the fourth was the massive Cathedral Metropolitana.

Traffic around the Zocalo seemed to drive by its own rules, a chaos that seemed to work. They crossed the five lanes and made their way to the left towards the Cathedral. Karen's awareness was drawn to the massive bell towers. Outside were numbers of people selling goods. They all walked into the cathedral together. The ceiling was massive. So high that she couldn't even guess how high. The whole structure was more than impressive. Karen was again overcome with a sense of awe; this time, the love for a God that she didn't believe in was overwhelming. The people who made this, made it with so much love and devotion to a God she had never bothered to know about. The feeling of dedication and connectedness to the sacred wonder silenced her. Again tears formed in Karen's eyes. The more she walked in the massive temple to God, the more humbled and emotional she felt. It truly was a sacred space in proportions that stunned her mind. Michelle walked up to her.

"This church is much more touristy, isn't it? It definitely doesn't have the same feeling as the other one," she said loudly.

Karen bit back her tears, and tried to hide the emotion breaking in her heart. Those words couldn't have been further from her experience. Shocked disbelief suddenly distanced her from her friend.

Just then, the cathedral bells began to toll midday. Their vibrations echoed throughout the massive building and as the momentum built, the vibrations began resonating in the girls' bodies. On and on the tolling went, and Karen began to laugh like a child at the experience. The others began to laugh with her. Their bodies were like tuning instruments, tuning into the tones of the bells. They all looked at each other and started yelling above the noise. Karen wanted to stay in that experience, but at the same time, she wanted to be outside seeing the bells being rung. They all had the same desire.

Together they ran through the church, out the side doors and into the paved yard in front of the building. Hundreds of other people were also standing in the yard, watching the bells.

Filled with childlike wonder, all of them strained their heads back as far as they could to see the bells. Then, as suddenly as it started, the bells stopped.

They all looked at each other and laughed again. Why had they done that? What had happened?

The crowd began to disperse as the moment ended, so the girls continued on their busy schedule of sights they wanted to see that day.

They passed the market stalls on the way to one of the massive buildings that edged the square. It was Mexico's parliament building. A regal balcony where the president came out to address the people overlooked the square and the enormous Mexican flag symbolized the pride of the nation.

Inside was calm and quiet; a contrast to the hectic life outside. They followed the small flow of people that lead up the stairs to the second story, viewing the murals that were the main attraction in the building. The detailed paintings filled the entire wall, from floor to ceiling, with scenes from pre-Hispanic tribal life through the twentieth century life of industries and unions.

Other murals graced the walls. Karen looked in fascination at the next painting. At first she didn't understand what it was, but then she realized she was looking at a market scene of the mighty Aztecan city called Mexico, pronounced Meh-hee-co. In the background of the scene was the city itself. It was a massive stone city with many temples and buildings. Karen stared at the picture and a strange sense of familiarity came over her. As she looked at the faces of the pre-Hispanic people and at the pictures of the buildings, she felt like she knew it. Beside them was a tour group with a guide. She walked over to him and asked if he could explain the meaning of the picture to her.

"You are looking at the sacred city of the *Aztecas* that this city is built over," he said. "These people were renowned for their warrior skills and for their rich culture. This picture shows a culture of huge wisdom that just disappeared five hundred years ago. The artist's name is Diego, and he did a great job of showing us what that great city really was like. Even the Spaniards were surprised to see such a civilization when they arrived. The legend goes that the *Azteca* warriors knew the invasion was coming so they simply surrendered to it, to make it as effortless as possible. You have heard of the famous gold the Spaniards were after but never found? Well, that was because it was in the *Aztecas'* hearts. They knew a profound wisdom that exceeds what we try to know today, a wisdom that was lost as soon as the invaders came. We say it's lost, but many believe it was hidden until a time when the world would respect it and use it in its pure form, and not for selfish personal power." He paused and looked in wonder and respect at the painting.

"The pyramids that have survived are still a mystery, but what we have found out about them is very surprising. Many people call them "ruins," but they are not ruins. When you visit them, and you are still and filled with respect, you can feel they are very much alive. They are still doing what they were built to do. They are pumping out energy. The reason they were built, and what they are designed to do, is completely beyond most humans' comprehension. It's so huge and powerful. It is amazing the universe has waited all this time for humanity to stop being so selfish. And the original people are still there maintaining it all. It's just beyond the conscious human eye at the moment. That is because most of us resonate with an energy that's so low. But humanity is waking up. *Mexico* is waking up. We will bring it all back. It's destined to be so."

The guide looked towards his group, and indicated he needed to move on. Karen thanked him and moved away slightly.

She continued to stare at the picture. She knew it. Something inside her remembered those steep stairs leading down from the temple, as if she had walked them before. She had a flash of memory, being in white, of walking in sacred silence as she descended down the steps. Something inside her recognized the people's features. Something inside her remembered the sacred way of life. Right now, though, it felt like a dream. Karen kept this to herself, thinking, *How could I start to say these things to my friends? What would I try to say?*

The girls wanted to head to the south of the city, to an area they had been told to see called Coyoacan. It was renowned for its beauty. They waved down two taxis and again were traveling across the city. This was no ordinary city to drive through. Traffic was always busy and the distances were long. It was a common thing to take an hour driving from one part to another, so you could lose a great part of your day in traveling, even on the freeways.

Suddenly they were pulling off the busy main avenue and onto a narrow side street.

"Is this it?" All the girls peered out the window. "Yes, this is Coyoacan," said the taxi driver.

The whole atmosphere had changed. The buildings looked narrow and colonial. They held the feel of the Spanish occupation of hundreds of years ago. The taxi passed by a few narrow streets, then stopped. The streets had suddenly opened out into a huge square with paved walkways and trees. The girls all piled out of the taxis and stood on the pavement, looking around them. Coyoacan was famous for its weekend markets. But this was midweek and they had no idea what they would be presented with.

As soon as Karen stepped out of the taxi, she heard it. She looked around her trying to see what direction the drumming was coming from. The others stood on the curb talking and discussing what to do. They were oblivious to the sounds or to the excitement it was creating in her.

"Let's find a coffee shop," said Kelly. "One with good coffee, this time."

"No," Karen said, already walking towards the noise. "Let's go over there and see what the drumming is all about. I want to find out what it is." She glanced back to see if they were following her. They all looked at each other and shrugged in indifference.

"OK. We can do that first." They followed her across the square. Karen walked quickly. She didn't want the drumming to finish before they got there.

To the average tourist, it might not have looked like much. There were no traditional costumes, there were no bright colors, there were no souvenirs being sold. The other girls had a quick look at the scene and were ready for something else. They were in Coyoacan; they had to see and do all that they could.

But to Karen it was mesmerizing. The drumming was primitive and tribal. She was drawn to it. About twenty or thirty people had formed a large circle. They were dressed in normal modern street clothes, but all were native Mexicans. Karen looked at each face and saw they all had the facial characteristics of the Mayan or Aztec people. They held a pride for their people, for their cultures and for an almost forgotten custom. Their dancing was highly energetic. The people leapt from side to side, they stomped and they twirled all in time together, without a word. Just to the drumbeat.

Their movements went on almost continuously for over thirty minutes. Some of the dancers swayed, not leaping so intensely as others. Some of them were sweating profusely. A handful of the dancers had total body control and were unaffected by the intensity of the dancing. Yet, as she looked at their faces Karen noticed an intense concentration, and a total ease at the same time. Their movements were precise and controlled and they weren't puffing or faltering at all. They were totally present and in tune with what they were doing. Karen was enthralled. The other girls fell into the background as her awareness became one with the dancers. She wanted to know what it was, who they were, why they were doing this.

What did it mean? She felt an urgency arise in her as the need to know grew. She felt like she would miss the experience of a lifetime if she didn't have that information.

Then, suddenly, like a gentle cloud, the urgency and the need to know slipped away. Karen relaxed into right now and became one with the meaning of the moment. She didn't need the questions to be answered to her head's satisfaction. She felt them being answered in her heart. Her heart knew. Her heart recognized something beyond mere information. As the drumming continued she saw the perfection in the universe doing everything to get her to this place, for this moment, for her to experience this.

What amazing perfection! She wouldn't even be in this country if it weren't for her friends. Suddenly she recognized the perfection of this holiday with the girls. They had helped to bring her here, for this moment.

Her awareness moved with the dancers, her soul sang with the primal drumbeat, and she couldn't take her eyes off two of them in particular. She saw the precision of their moves and the sacredness of their connection to the dancing. She also had the awareness that she knew them. She knew it was impossible, but as she watched them, she knew that she knew them. That they reminded her of something. Something buried long ago. Something that had never been forgotten, just overlooked. Something that still existed in her. Something that burned in her. Their whole energy, their look, reminded her of an ancient time, another lifetime that was still alive in her. They were awakening her reason to be here. They were reminding her of her purpose, her bigger purpose.

The drumming stopped. The dancers stopped. A lady walked into the center of the circle, holding a silver bowl. Smoke began to rise, white and dense, from the bowl. She lifted it above her head. The smoke floated to Karen; she could smell it, sweet and earthy. The smell reminded her of something in the past, the sacred smell of copal. As the resin smoldered, the lady lifted the bowl to the north, the south, the east and the west. All the dancers moved in the direction that she did, also honoring whatever it was she was honoring.

Someone from the crowd of bystanders wanted to leave and went to make a shortcut through the circle and between the dancers. As he hurried unconsciously through, the dancers he walked between started in shock, responding a few seconds too late to stop him. Then they looked at each other, shrugged and closed their eyes in unison. To Karen it looked like they were saying a silent prayer for the behavior and for the interruption of the circle.

Karen then realized these dancers were moving within a sacred circle. Their movements were creating union with the greatest of energies. A union with the greatest of intelligence. Each of them was creating union with God. To these people it might have a different name, but it was the same intelligence. It was the same force that created the rains, that gave life and that took life. She suddenly realized the greatness of what she was watching. She was witnessing the dancers' communion with God.

Her friends didn't see that at all. They had been sitting there and talking for half an hour and now they were cold and bored. They hadn't come to Coyoacan to be bored. They wanted to go. They all got up to leave.

Karen felt like she walked between two worlds as they moved away from the dancers. As they crossed the square to the area where the restaurants were, she felt like her body was operating on this earth right now, while another part of her was somewhere else. Certainly in another place and perhaps in another time.

They got their table and ordered their drinks. The rest of the girls fell back into chatter about their holiday, remembering, speculating and gossiping, but Karen stared out into the square. The drumming had started up again.

All at once the building, the table and her friends faded into the background and the other reality took its place. Both worlds were co-existing at the same time, but it was the totally different world that dominated her senses.

A woman appeared in front of her. She looked like the woman who had been with the dancers a few minutes before. She held the bowl with the smoldering copal in it. The wisps of white smoke rising from the bowl were thick and the smell of the copal was dense and sweet. The woman was solemn, her energy that of intense observation and sacredness.

Karen noticed the woman's face. Her eyes held her gaze. The woman had dark makeup streaked across her eyes and forehead. She had a headdress on, made from long feathers and fresh leaves. But the eyes were so intense and powerful. The woman held the bowl to Karen in offering. The vision expanded and Karen suddenly realized she was dressed the same as the woman. She also had makeup across her eyes, a large headdress and was dressed totally in white. Karen recognized that her presence was one of great importance. The woman offering the bowl to her was offering a sign of spiritual respect. In fact Karen knew that she was the holder of great wisdom, a leader of some sort.

The vision expanded again and she recognized pyramids, ancient stones and the presence of other great teachers who also held the wisdom of these people. As she accepted the bowl, she instantly knew that they were protecting their knowledge. They were performing this ceremony to seal this knowledge from the world, for they knew the invaders were approaching. They knew these invaders could destroy this path they guarded to the Gods. It was up to these people to protect the path of wisdom, and so they were going to seal it away until the time came when it could be used again.

Karen blinked and looked around. The drumming had stopped. She definitely was back in the coffee shop with her friends and it was late. The customers were all leaving. She looked around, wondering if her friends thought she had been acting strangely. Her half-finished cup of coffee was in front of her, so she knew she had been drinking from it, yet she had no recollection of being in the coffee shop at all. The other experience had been so vivid to her, she knew it was real. She knew she had been there.

What was the point though? *Why am I supposed to remember other lives like that, lives of spiritual importance?* She asked herself, confused. But as soon as that thought floated through her mind, the answer immediately filled her being. The answer was right there. She knew the answer in her heart.

It was time for her to wake up.

It was time for her to do what she was really here to do. She already knew she was sick of the life she had been living. She already knew she couldn't continue living that way. She felt the pain of compromising every time she backed down from what she knew, for her friends' sakes. She knew there was more for her. She'd recognized it for a long time, but hadn't wanted to take steps in that direction. She'd been afraid of change, but now she couldn't ignore it. Too much had happened to her over the last week. Steve, the guy she had met, had opened her up to a world of ideas she had never experienced before. She now had the ideas, but she wanted the experience. And, she'd just had a vision that told her the experience could be real.

She'd once had that experience of the connection to God, and now it was time for her to experience it again. She knew with all her heart that was true. She knew she was here for a bigger reason than the one she had been living. Now she recognized just how big it was. Karen looked out into the dark square of Coyoacan and spoke to the universe.

I'm ready, was the thought she let float out from her heart, out into the source of all. *I'm ready to do what I came here to do.*

People choose the pleasant over the good,
Think of your own life and
think when you have chosen what was okay
over what was good.
Our lives are full of compromise.
People are addicted to pain and suffering.
But everybody yearns
to be united with God.

M.K.I.

Almira

Almira sat quietly and watched the people walk into the room. The married lady called Mary had arrived early; Almira recognized her from their meeting outside the grocery store. Two young ladies had just walked in and were also seating themselves. Almira loved these evenings. She'd been teaching for a few years now, and class after class had gotten more powerful and rich for her.

She didn't think of herself as a teacher. She was simply someone who now had a greater experience of life and wanted to share that with others. The joy, perfection and sacredness she felt in each moment was so great it was natural to offer that for everyone else also.

It was such a joy to meet the people in these evenings. She knew each person here wanted something more. They wanted to know if it was possible to live a different way, wanted to know if there was some meaning in their lives. Every person realized at some level their lives weren't fulfilling them in the ways they'd wanted. It was common for humans to stunt their growth in many unconscious ways, and pride was one of them. Admitting their lives weren't what they wanted was a huge step. Everyone sitting in this room was curious to see what Almira would say and if she had the answer. Whether they knew it or not, they were looking for someone to say, "Yes, I've found it."

Almira remembered the first time she had gone to one of these evenings. She had gone because a friend had invited her to go, but she had been filled with resistance. She didn't believe her life needed to change. She would have told herself it was okay, even if it wasn't.

She remembered the longing she'd felt when she saw the two teachers, and had spent the evening trying to deny that feeling. The words and the honesty the teachers had spoken with had lit a flame of desire for the truth in her. She had tried to ignore it, but she couldn't turn back. Trying to do so only grew more and more painful as time went on.

What she had learnt continued to grow in her experience. What they'd said was true; it was real to live your life in continual joy and peace. There came a point in her growth when she realized that what she'd discovered and what she experienced had to be given away. She wanted to share this with others. She wanted others to know there was a choice. That the other way of living wasn't necessary, and was painful. She wanted them to know they could easily reclaim who they really were and watch the happiness flood back into their lives.

What a gift. What a beautiful thing to share.

Almira sat watching these wonderful people who were curious for more. She knew she had the key that could open the door to their freedom. But they were the ones who had to recognize it. They were the ones who had to make the choice.

Sitting in front of the now twenty or so people who had been arriving over the past fifteen minutes, Almira was totally aware of the people moving into the room, seating themselves and quietly whispering with those they knew. Yet most of her awareness was submerged into a well of infinite space, a void of emptiness, which contained eternal peace. A space that joy and laughter bubbled up from. So still. So silent. So eternal. The essence of creation, the purpose of the universe resided within this presence. A love that was so real, so powerful and so solid. It was the pureness of creation.

Almira sat in bliss, with that essence radiating out of her and touching the hearts of everyone ready to recognize it. She knew that she didn't have to do anything except offer her hand to those who wanted it.

Dave meets a monk

Dave had been expecting something else. Actually, he didn't know what he was expecting. He just knew that this was way too normal. When he'd heard there would be monks doing a talk, he had visualized saffron robes, shaved heads, clanking bells, burning incense, groupies, and weird music. He'd been curious, but he hadn't wanted to get sucked into anything. He'd been angry with himself for wanting to go.

He was angry a lot these days.

He had returned from his trip to the Islands and the restlessness that had sent him there in the first place continued to gnaw into his heart. If he hadn't been aware of it before, he was totally aware of it now. He hadn't found his peace or the meaning of life from his trip; instead, the questions just seemed to plague him more. There were more questions and no answers. Nothing seemed to hold meaning for him. Nothing seemed to bring any sort of satisfaction. His trip had made him more frustrated, not less.

As much as he loved the Islands, he longed to return to his security of the city, yet when he got back to work he felt alienated by it. The energy there seemed negative. He wasn't experiencing the passion of the corporate world. He felt like he was on automatic, just going to work and going home. Where did all the passion for what he'd been doing go? Nothing seemed to give him peace. He seemed to feel hollow and alone.

Time continued to tick on. Moment after moment. Chance after chance. Some of those moments seemed obvious, and some made absolutely no sense. Still they unfolded into days, and slowly into months. Often he seemed caught in what his life had been. Dave compared now to back then, and now just didn't seem good enough. There was suddenly a void as big as his being that he couldn't seem to get out of. This life seemed like a cruel dream of hope being replaced with no hope. There was nothing and no one around him that seemed to mean anything. He felt like he could get up and walk away and no one would notice. Nothing meant anything. So, what was the point of it all? Why this job, this town, these people and even this life. Why?

He remembered his grandfather telling him every piece of the puzzle had its purpose. Every piece has its place. We just don't see it. Dave wanted to see it. He wanted to understand. He felt like screaming at the world. He was tired of feeling like he was fighting all the time. Why was this world full of stupid people? Why didn't they care? Why did he care? Why was he always angry these days?

He drove up to the address he'd scribbled on a piece of paper. He parked his car and looked at the normal house in the very normal looking neighborhood. He sat for a moment, sighed, then grabbed his jacket and got out of the car. He walked up the concrete path to the front door and rang the doorbell. He was already on defense. A lady opened the door and gave him a warm smile. He didn't smile back. He glared at her with mistrust and suspicion and automatically judged her as false. Too nice. No normal person was that open and nice. A scowl crossed his face, and doubt crept into his mind. What was he doing here?

The woman guided him into the house, and into the living room, before he could seriously consider turning around. There was already a group of people in there.

He quickly scanned the room, looking for the robed monks. Instead of shaven heads, his eyes fell on the person sitting in the front of the room. She was a normal looking person. Normal looking, but with something that definitely wasn't normal. The woman was wearing normal clothes; in fact, they were nice trendy clothes. He stared at her and she casually met his gaze. She stared back but there was something that he had never seen before. Something he had rarely experienced. Her gaze held power, security and a kind of detachment, but also a strength and a love, an unconditional love.

Dave didn't know where to look. He instantly felt at home and comfortable, but his mind said no. Most times when girls look at you for a long moment, they were checking you out and flirting with you. This lady's stare held none of that. There was no desire for him, no secret messages, no interest. It was maybe the first time he had looked at a woman and seen this. She had a total contentment within herself, and didn't need anything from anyone. Dave was instantly confused. He was attracted to what she had, but he didn't know what it was. He knew it wasn't sexual... but what could it be?

The timeless, detached gaze rested on him for a while, and then the woman closed her eyes in silent meditation.

Dave was struck by her silence. No other woman in his life was so calm and sure of herself. Every female he knew was always trying to impress him. This woman was obviously experiencing something else. There was something much greater than what he'd come across so far in his life, and here it was sitting right in front of him.

Dave felt his painful search come to a halt as he watched her. The curiosity that had become as painful as a raging fire over the last months stopped. He watched the woman and found the tension drain from his being. He sat in the chair and waited for the evening to begin.

The Teacher resides in the Silence,
eternal and immovable.
The student evolves and approaches the Teacher.
And as the student meets the Teacher in the Silence,
the true Teaching and guidance is there.

M.K.I.

———— ————

Who's in the living room?

Karen looked around at the familiar faces in the room. Some surprised her… but the one that surprised her the most was her girlfriend Kelly. Karen had mentioned to all her friends she was going out this evening. She hadn't expected any of them to be interested. She had hoped that her closest friend, Michelle, might have wanted to come. But Michelle had made up some excuses at the last minute. Once again, Karen had been left feeling disappointed with who she thought her friends were. She had wanted a friend to explore this spiritual direction with her. But she seemed to be her own best friend, again.

A week ago, Karen had walked into Starbucks to get a coffee. It was a busy morning. There were people everywhere. Karen idly looked around the people as she waited for her coffee. She liked to try to guess their stories. Who were they and what had brought them to this place this morning. When she got her drink, she moved to a table to sit down, but hesitated and moved into the bookstore and to the magazines. She walked slowly down the isles of magazines, scanning the covers for anything interesting. There were the usual magazines on glamour, gossip and beautiful people. She picked one up out of habit and flicked through it looking at the pictures. It bored her, so she put it back. She sipped her coffee, but it was still a bit hot for her liking.

Then a magazine caught her attention. It had a picture of the Dalai Lama on the cover. His eyes stared at her with love and humor. She looked at him for a few moments. Such a beautiful face. He was wearing the saffron robes of the monk. A symbol of a life dedicated to spirituality. Everything about him emanated peace. She put her coffee down on the floor and thumbed through the pages, looking for the article about him. Every page in the magazine was showing pictures of people in yoga positions or meditating in beautiful surroundings. She found the article about him and began reading the highlighted words. *'How to live in this world with a connection to the Divine. Discover the sacredness in you. How to have positive living with harmony, peace, joy.'* The whole article was filled with beautiful words.

Suddenly, her whole being changed. She felt a rush of excitement flood through her. It was as if the magazine was talking to her personally.

On the shelves were other magazines on inner peace, meditation and wholesome living. She grabbed at them and began flicking through them all. There was so much information. Where was she going to begin? She felt like a sponge finally receiving the water to soak up. Why had she never seen these magazines before?

With a new purpose, she selected three magazines and put the rest back. She picked up her coffee and made her way to the area in the bookstore titled "Self Help." She cringed at the name and at the idea of needing help, but she began scanning the shelves of books. There were so many. So many subjects. She had no idea what she was really after. Her intense joy began to slip away and confusion began to take over. She looked at the prices of some of the books that appealed to her, and she winched at the thought of spending the money. She looked at the bookshelf, feeling dejected and alone. What was she supposed to do? What was she supposed to know? Reality overtook her excitement. She had a few bills to pay this week, so she shouldn't go wasting money on silly books and magazines. She looked at the magazines in her hand and sighed. If only someone could tell her, guide her. She picked out one magazine and left the other two where she had just been standing, and made her way to the counter.

As she stood in line she doubted if she even really needed this magazine. It was ten dollars and that was money she could put on her Visa bill. As these thoughts were running through her mind, she glanced at the notice board by the counter. There were flyers and mini posters of events coming up in town. She started to read them. She looked at the date on one and noticed it was in a week's time. An evening talk in town, by monks. She started to read the brief information again. *Change your life by changing yourself. The simplicity of the reality.*

She paused and subconsciously let the words sink into her heart. *The simplicity of the reality.* Her heart recognized the energy in the words and said, 'yes.' Her skeptical head had doubts, but she found herself writing the details down in her little pocket diary.

Over the next week she mentioned the evening to her girlfriends a couple of times. She really wanted to go. No one else shared her passion at all. Michelle had said she was interested, but made excuses at the last minute.

That was when Kelly had stepped into the picture. She had said she was curious about that stuff, and then added she didn't have anything else better to do. Karen was totally amazed Kelly would be the one sitting beside her at the talk. This was the topic, which she had often loudly declared to be "full of shit."

Even now as they were sitting in the house, Karen was glancing at Kelly with doubt. She didn't want Kelly to laugh at her and ruin her evening.

Kelly grinned back at her and shrugged. "I don't know why I'm here, either. It's not really my thing. I'm not really sure what my thing is. Maybe you and I have more in common than you know."

Karen stared at Kelly. She was wondering if she was speaking the truth or mocking her. Kelly looked totally sincere. For the first time since they had been friends Karen saw something real in Kelly. She saw beyond the images and the masks Kelly lived through. Maybe Kelly and she had the same desire. Maybe Karen was just more open about it. For the first time Karen's heart really expanded as she looked at her friend. They were after the same thing. They were the same. Two young women trying to make sense out of their lives. Two lives molded by the conditions of society. They were influenced by the fashions, by relationships, and by everything the magazines threw at them, constantly. Lives conditioned by popularity, approval, doing what people expected of them. They had no idea who they really were and what they wanted, and instead lived on the roller coaster of the quickly changing world.

Looking at Kelly now in an environment where she didn't have to prove herself, she seemed real and genuine. She was searching for answers, just like Karen.

"Isn't it funny how things work out?" thought Karen. "I would never have guessed this in a million years."

"You know what I think?" Kelly continued in a casual manner, "is that I admire you for how you want to go out and do something and change things. I see that in you all the time. But what I also see is how annoyed you get so quickly with us and other people. I get pretty annoyed with other people also," she laughed, "but I'm pretty happy with who I am. But I know there is more to life than what I know, that's why I'm here.

"I'm not putting you down, so don't go all defensive on me. I'm just saying you need to stop judging others so harshly." She paused. "I might sound like a hypocrite, but I see people as being okay where they are at. And everyone needs to move on when they are ready. You can't go around hitting people over the head with all the spiritual mumbo jumbo. Like, look at me. I'm here because I want to be, not because of what you have been talking about for the last month or any other reason." She looked at Karen and laughed. "Who knows? Maybe I have been listening to you. That is supposed to be a compliment. Does it sound like one?"

They looked at each other, then they both started to laugh. Karen looked at her friend and shook her head in pretend disbelief. She knew what she was saying, and she knew it wasn't intended to be derogatory. That was just the way her friend saw the world and lived in it.

Karen leaned back into the couch she was sitting on, a smile on her lips. What an interesting thought. Imagine if all the people in her life were playing their parts, helping her and themselves to become more spiritually aware. Maybe some people didn't need the knowledge, like she did, but were becoming more conscience just by living life. It was a nice thought. Suddenly she could love her friends more for being who they were. At the same time, she knew she was here because she was doing this for herself.

She glanced around the room again. There were faces she knew, other faces that were familiar to her, and faces she didn't know at all. There were about twenty people seated in the room. Some knew each other and were talking. Others were sitting quietly by themselves, waiting for the evening to begin.

Sitting quietly and calmly in a chair at the front of the room was a lady who looked slightly older than Karen. The presence of peace around her was huge. Her slight smile was real, warm and loving. Her eyes held no fear. They were calm and filled with laughter. Confidently, she sat still, waiting for everyone to arrive. She looked like she needed nothing from anyone and wasn't afraid of anything. All in the most loving and humble way.

Karen watched her. Was this it? Were the words to come out of this lady's mouth what she had been aching for? Was it what she had been wanting in her life? Karen had already decided that she wanted what that lady had. She had recognized something that didn't have words.

Impatiently, she waited for the evening to begin.

As long as you believe in the possibility of suffering,
you will weep for the agony of this world.
As you evolve you will learn that it's your beliefs
that are making your Universe so.
Your judgements of good and evil,
acceptance and pain.
It's your belief in suffering that is
creating your Universe as it is.

Almira speaks

————— ✦ —————

"When the mind is stunned by awe, by wonderment, it stills," said Almira. "It stills from the constant hammering of jumbled thoughts it is usually trapped in. Those thoughts can be so constant there is no room for the wonderment of life anymore.

"People are so busy. Even when their bodies are still, their minds are still busy thinking. They miss the beauty of life. They miss life. Instead of living a life in awe of itself, we live a life caught in what we should do or what we should have done.

"When you start to realize how most people are living, and how life is supposed to be lived, at first the enormity of the sadness and pain for human unconsciousness can be overwhelming. Then it becomes the greatest joke. Most people on this planet are walking around in total unconsciousness, totally asleep. They have fleeting moments of peace and stillness, but they totally overlook it and think they have to be entertained by their senses. A great day is judged by how much you have laughed. A great time is extreme happiness stimulated by something. Everyone lives on this emotional roller coaster.

"People have forgotten the calm inner bliss. The peace and strength. They have forgotten who they are."

Dave had never heard it said like this before. It was so simply put. So real, and sounding so easy to change and access.

Dave looked at Almira for a long time. It was one of the great mysteries of life, and this lady was speaking as if it was easy. It was just overlooked. He had envisioned long years in a monastery, special powers being unleashed by mental training. Enduring harsh conditions, which could nearly kill him. And she's saying that it is because we think! Everybody thinks all the time. What's so special about that?

Sue felt enveloped with a warm sense of security. Everything the lady was saying made sense. Almira could have been talking about Sue's life. All of it.

Mary was hanging onto Almira's every word. Everything made sense. It was all so practical, that it all made sense. How easy it all sounded. How exciting.

Karen had begun the evening in fear. She was so worried about having Kelly sitting beside her. She kept looking at her friend hoping to God she wasn't going to say something really rude, like Kelly had often done to her. Slowly she had relaxed and began listening fully to what Almira was saying. Almira had been using scientific data to explain what she was saying. How did she know all of this? Why didn't everyone know this? It all seemed so obvious and true. How had she missed it?

"So much can be achieved by the human," Almira continued. "People who strive for only one goal experience that: athletes, businessmen. They know what it means to put all they are behind one goal and go for it. Many people have spent their whole lives, years and years, striving to expand the abilities of the body. And maybe they do achieve it. Many books tell stories of yogis and siddhas who can raise their body temperature at will, breathe fire, manifest objects or do amazing martial arts. But are they free from the pain and the suffering? Are they free from the constant changes in the changing world around us? They may or may not know it. Often they are proud of their abilities and show them off. If that is so, then they are identified with them and are thinking! So, they are still in prison. The prison cell is the mind. It may look a bit fancier, but they are still not free.

"The greatest pain of the human is the belief they are separate from the greatest force. That they are less than. Religions and beliefs teach that mankind needs to prove itself. That we are less than God. We spend our lives trying to prove ourselves and trying to find out... something."

Kelly was riveted to what the lady was saying. Almira had been talking for a while now and the room was totally focused on her. Kelly had started out this evening filled with skepticism, but that had dissolved as the evening moved on. What this lady was saying, was that it was about you. It was up to you. The choice was yours. It was about your moment-by-moment experience of life. You have the power of choice for that.

There was no way Kelly was going to join a group or anything like that. In fact, that was exactly the reason why she reacted so strongly when Karen or anyone else started speaking about that spiritual stuff. She wanted to be herself and that was exactly what this lady was talking about. She was intrigued. She wanted more of life. The emotional roller coaster was so familiar to her. She could totally relate to that comment. And she was sick of it. She wanted her own strength. She wanted to flourish into her own true self.

This seemed so precise and direct. There was no need to be anything except who she really was. She knew this was true.

She also totally understood what Almira was saying earlier in the evening, that the habit of the mind was often so strong or so unconscious that most people just can't return to a place of continual freshness and innocence automatically. Most people need a teaching, a tool or a technique to follow, to help them. And most importantly, they need the guidance from someone who has walked the path before them. Why? Because we are breaking a habit and pride is the biggest drawback. Humility and humbleness are the fast tracks to receiving the gifts of the universe.

"One time, I was at a big gathering as a guest speaker on meditation", Almira continued. "Before my talk began, I was casually talking to some people. One person overheard me mention the words 'unconditional love,' and had to express his opinion to me. He said there was no way in the world unconditional love exists. He said we had conditions on everything. We had conditions on our partners. They had to treat us a certain way. We cared what they did or didn't do. We had conditions and expectations on our family. We had a lot of conditions and expectations on our friends. We even had expectations on our pet dog!

"Love had to have conditions," he said to me. "Unconditional love couldn't exist."

"I agreed with him. I agreed most people thought the way he did and only knew of love with conditions. They treated love as something people or things *deserved* and so that was why they didn't experience anything else.

"To most people, that is what love is. You demand, you expect and then you hurt when it isn't fulfilled. It's a love that has limits. It's a love of taking and of needing. It's a love that feels like it could end at any moment. It's scary and unstable and we don't trust it because we don't want to get hurt. Yet, we want it, but it seems so insecure and fleeting. It's an illusion of love that is based in fear, so really, only the fear exists.

"Always, if we try to take love from the world to fulfill us, we feel that restriction and pain. There is no way it can fulfill us. It can't. We desire to be loved totally. We want to love the world fully, yet we can't. We don't know how to. We search and search without finding the true love. Then we come to a point when we believe that this is as good as it will get, so we might as well put up with what we have. But there is more, so much more.

"Unconditional love is the love that comes from within you. It is solid, eternal and knows no limits. It knows no conditions. It's like the rain. It doesn't choose who not to fall on. Instead it falls on everybody and all things equally. It sees no reason not to. It doesn't have judgments and expectations. Instead, it's the pure love of life itself. It's what holds and binds all life together. It's not fleeting. Instead it's stronger than steel. It knows no end as it's the source of all things. And it is you. That is who you really are. "You don't know that, simply because you have chosen to look outside of yourself for that satisfaction. We look in relationship after relationship. We look in job after job. We might look in churches and beliefs. And if those teachings point to a God outside of us, we will still feel the emptiness and continue to search. We might look for approval, with friends, in assets. We might even try to escape this world with drug use or alcohol abuse. This is a chemical way to try to destroy our limitations and inhibitions. We might even travel endlessly or live for our holidays every year. I can relate to a lot of these examples, because that is what I was doing, but I didn't know why I was doing it. Because I didn't know there was anything else.

"We live in a world of separation. We feel separated from our home, separated from each other and definitely separated from God. We are taught separation in school and are encouraged to compete individually rather than learn as a team.

"Anytime we feel afraid, insecure or abandoned it comes back to the same belief, and that is we feel separated from the source of who we are.

We feel separated from our Truth, our reason for being here. That is why we ask those questions, like 'Who am I?' and 'Why am I here?' and even 'What am I really supposed to be doing?'

"It's just a belief. It's just a thought! But that one thought is THE reason for all the suffering, wrong doing and anguish experienced on this planet. It is the reason.

"To dissolve that idea of separation could seem like an arduous task of repairing years of damage, but it's not. It's just an idea. We can dissolve it at anytime, and instead experience oneness, unity and perfection in our world and with each other.

"Most importantly, we can experience completeness and oneness with the unconditional love within ourselves and all things. That unconditional love is God."

They all sat in silence for a while. There was nothing that was needed to be said. Almira's words hung thickly in the air as if they were painted there. The words resonated in their hearts. They didn't want to break the spell.

"We can even have the belief, which seems like such a noble belief, that we need to heal the world and the people around us," Almira began. "So many people are viewing the world and the population as imperfect and needing help. This is true, in a sense. We need to become aware something needs changing to make the choices to move into more conscious ways of living, being and experiencing life. But as we see the imperfection, it's a mirror of the imperfection in ourselves. Now, I didn't understand this for the longest time. I could see the problems and the pollution and the destruction on the planet. I could see the pain in people, so how could that be a mirror of myself? I thought the greatest compassion and purpose was to help heal everything. But to heal something outside of what we perceive ourselves to be, well, we are still focusing on the imperfection and not the perfection.

"Said another way, if you heal someone's disease, the reason why they created the disease is still in place. They still have the ability to recreate the disease through their own ignorance and most people do. So the real cause hasn't been addressed. Someone gets depressed because they don't like their job. So they change jobs. They get depressed again, and again.

The real reason why they are getting depressed isn't really about the jobs they are in. It's because of their attitude, their mentality, and so the same symptoms get repeated over and over again. It's the same with people who seem to continuously get into relationships that don't work. You can keep changing the relationships, but it's not about the other person or the relationship itself. It's about the mentality of the person who keeps creating the disharmony.

Most people are continuously trying to change the world and the people around them with the hope that then they will be happy. What we have to discover is that it is up to us to change ourselves. We have the power to erase all our unconscious reactive patterns and negative beliefs that we hold in place. Then a whole new world magically unfolds before our eyes. A world of perfection and joy. A world where we live and breathe that perfection and experience that love.

"What everyone is doing," Almira continued, "is searching, and the reason for that search is to find that pure love. We will never find it outside of ourselves. We will only find it within.

"When we start to experience that peace and love inside, it's a natural process for that love to expand outward into our lives and into our world. Totally pure, totally unconditional, without attachments or expectations.

"It's the love of giving for the pure joy of giving to life. It's the love of giving because you love yourself and your world. It's the love that is endless and self-sustaining. It needs nothing and no one, but loves all.

"To love your partner, family and anyone on the street from that wholeness of loving yourself is beyond these words. It is total contentment. It's totally full and complete. It's how everyone should be living and loving their life.

"The greatest joke is that it's all an illusion. There is nothing to find. Nothing to become. There is nothing missing. You just don't recognize who you really are, and think that you are less. There is your eternal pain right there!"

Dave sat looking at Almira. A love, an intense love, started to fill every cell in his body. So much love he wanted to cry. In front of him sat the most amazing person he had ever met. He had never met someone with such humility, but such inner strength. She had incredible passion for what she was doing. She was absolutely committed to what she was doing. She had the ability to touch everyone's heart through her own honesty. She didn't need to impress. She didn't care whether you stayed or left. She didn't need anyone, yet she loved everyone warmly and unconditionally.

Dave had never experienced such honesty before. He felt ashamed he wasn't like that. He had fought and scrambled his way through life for a long time.

Here in front of them all was a beauty beyond words, the beauty of Truth, just radiating from her heart and eyes. He looked at her and found her staring back at him, a long, silent, detached, calm look that expressed nothing. He felt like she was looking into him and reading his thoughts.

"If one becomes quiet and still, it is very easy to feel what is being spoken, or what is *really* being spoken, and even what is being thought. There have only been a few people out of the whole global population who have discovered the Truth. A few have been guided to knowing who they really are, the divinity of which they are, and then been able to share that with anyone who wanted to listen. Often people did listen. But it was only a few who would then put what they had learnt into practice. These few often had to remove themselves from the common duties of the world as their practice didn't fit in. And so monasteries were built, often in remote places. Going to a monastery seems too extreme for most people today. A huge sacrifice of family and friends. Who wants to do that? So people would walk away from the greatest gift that could be offered to them at that time. Often they then condemned those who taught. Banished them, ridiculed them, and sometimes killed them!! All because they didn't understand. They were too blind to see. Too tied to ignorance. Too caught in violence and fear of mankind to even let the belief of love touch their hearts.

"In the last ten years, there has been a huge acceptance of spiritual concepts and ideas. Whether they seem airy-fairy, crazy, extreme, or real to you doesn't matter. The exciting thing is they started to appear and reappear, and now, today, it's a common thread in movies, books and conversation. People are totally aware and accepting at some level, that there is the possibility of more. Of something more for our lives. ESP, communicating with the dead, channeling information, reading tarot cards, studying the words of the Buddha, Zen masters, Osho, Sufi masters, people who claim to be enlightened, sages from India and China, Christian saints. It's all there, accessible and accepted.

"The path is straight and narrow. People who are drawn to me, whether they know it or not, are drawn to the Ultimate Truth. To the whole deal. They aren't here just to feel a little bit better. They aren't here to de-stress a little bit in their lives. They are here because they want it. They want to wake up. To realize that they are God. To recognize their enlightenment. It takes boldness and commitment. And the universe responds with giving you everything. Absolutely everything. This is the way we are supposed to live. So how can it be a strain or a torturous struggle? That's a myth. It's a joy to wake up into the greatness of who you are. It's amazing to realize what life is really all about. It's a joke to see humanity believing fear is real, necessary and always there. It's not true. It's simply not true. Anything that teaches that is a lie.

"Living anything less is missing the point of why we are here. We are here to experience life. We are here to make the choices to evolve more. We are here to realize the greatness of who we are, and to realize how easy it is. That's the whole answer to the question "why." The eternal question and the eternal answer.

"Nothing you have done has been wrong. All of it has gotten you to this point right now. It's been your own individual path of evolution, of waking up. Everything in your life has gotten you to here, and now you have heard the Truth. You now have heard the words that you are not separate from the God essence. Now you have to make the choices to experience that and then to live that.

"Those that recognize this, recognize the gem that has been theirs all along. What a joy. The experience never ceases to get better and better. The love continues to expand. The joy increases. The word "freedom" pales in comparison to the ever-expanding experience of freedom. The word "bliss" takes on a deeper and real meaning as you experience what bliss really is. The joy, love and magic become a permanent, fresh, won-drous, and natural part of your life.

"Who would want to say no to that? All that is required is a passion, a dedication and everything else is given to you. How easy.

"Everything that you have heard is true. Everything you've heard is yours. Everything you have recognized in me is for you.

"I have faith in you. The question is, do you have faith in yourself?"

"You can ask 'how can I bathe in peace
and absolute pristine stillness forever.
*How do I **do** that, and soon?'*
That's your choice."

M.K.I.

—————— ——————

Watching them leave

——— 🦋 ———

The end of the evening was always an interesting time. It might be the end of the talk, but it wasn't the end of Almira's night. Often, this was the beginning of the most important time of the night for her.

For the last couple of hours, she had shared her heart and her experience of how life could be lived and the ease with which it could be reclaimed by the individual. She included the scientific data that had graced the public over the last few years. It was the information we often heard and disregarded. When it gets presented all together, it's too obvious and real to be brushed aside.

None of this information was new. It had all been around for years. Actually the information had been known for thousands of years. In this day and age, we seem to think of the human race as advanced. Sure, we have advanced in technology, but we always come back to the same thing people have been coming back to forever. And that is to have a happier life. Ask anyone what their highest dream is for themselves. They might start with money and assets, but when asked what that will give them, the answer is always happiness or peace. It's the same desire of every human throughout time. We have all been searching for a way to reconnect to our heart.

In this day and age of machines and technology, the scientists of the past have been left behind. We have continued to scientifically study atoms and protons. And the quantum scientists are now studying things even smaller than that, which have intelligence by reacting to observation. Scientists are recognizing intelligence in the energy that becomes everything. They are recognizing there must be a greater intelligence that controls the energy and holds it all in balance. They haven't put a name to it, but the ancient cultures have always known about this intelligence; some refer to it as the Source, or the Father, or Chi.

Science has also pushed the boundaries as far away from earth as possible, trying to find answers out there. They discover time and time again the enormity of the universe and the energy and intelligence that holds it all in place. Ultimately it's the same intelligence that is in the trillions of cells inside our bodies that respond to our guidance. We guide with negativity and fear, and our cells respond. We guide with love and acceptance to ourselves and our world around us, and the cells respond to that, too. It's a fascinating universe, and it's happening within our bodies, within the trees in our area, within the building structures around us. The active intelligence is everywhere. Yet most of us never see the amazing world right in front of us.

Usually, in the face of all this information, some people would want to ask more questions, but are too shy to ask in the group. She made a point of looking out for those people. Often they would linger back, looking around or fiddling with their jackets. Sometimes there were people who just got up and left straight away. Almira wasn't bothered in the slightest. Everyone was walking their own path and was at different stages of their evolution. Some people needed to go away and think about the information they had just heard. Others just weren't ready for it. For some, their skepticism ran so deep they couldn't see beyond it, and that was okay. Her entire purpose was to hold the light, always, for them and for her.

It didn't often surprise her who wanted to linger back and talk to her. She had become intuitive to reading where people were in response to her talk. She could tell if they wanted to talk to her, or if they just wanted to get out the door. She could also notice the ones who recognized what she was saying. They would walk in curious and suddenly be as bright as neon lights. Their faces would transform into sunshine as their hearts recognized the truth and their minds understood it. It was so beautiful. People could be read like open books.

As usual, tonight there were a few people who got up, looked at their watches and left. Another couple came up to her, thanked her and left also. Some were slowly getting their coats and looking around. Almira watched them. She loved them. She was letting their hearts know they were welcome to approach her if they wanted to.

Almira smiled to herself. The energy in the room was wild. You could almost hear the battles going on in the people's minds. They wanted to stay, they wanted to ask more, but maybe they had better go. Some people's expressions were mirroring their thoughts. If only people realized how much was told in their energy. Maybe they would be more honest with themselves.

The owner of the house suddenly mentioned she was getting the tea and coffee out. The energy of the whole room changed instantly. People made up their minds whether to stay or go. They all recognized the invitation, and suddenly didn't have to make up an excuse.

Instantly there were three people asking her questions, then more came up to listen. Always in a class there would be at least one person ready to hear more.

She looked at the faces looking hopefully and curiously at her. The chit-chat had stopped and the focus was on the response she was going to give to a question. With lightning speed sadness moved through her. It was there and then gone. Why did humans have to do it like this? Why did we have to go through so much pain and separation? Why did we choose to endure so much suffering? Thank God there was another way. The bliss returned with more expansion and perfection as she looked into the eyes of the people sitting around her. "Oh, my God," she thought. So many beautiful hearts waiting to be opened. So many angels waiting to remember the greatness of who they are.

"I'm not different from you," she began. "I have lived a life on the roller coaster of emotions without knowing what to do with it all. And I have lived without knowing what direction I was going in. The only difference between you and me now, is that I know who I am. And I know who you really are. I no longer experience the confusion. It simply doesn't exist for me. I can teach you what I know and share with you my experience of living in wonderment of this universe in every moment. But you have to want it. The choice is yours."

The questions started to be aimed at her at rapid speed. She loved this. She loved people waking up. It was like a gate in the dam had been opened and the water was beginning to flood out. People were recognizing there was another way to live. They knew this in their hearts and were now asking the questions they needed to. They needed to dissolve all the doubt in their minds so they could experience the truth. The mind continues to judge, scrutinize and doubt. Even if her words were spoken well, it wasn't always about the words. Words were simply a way of communicating that everyone was used to. Everyone put so much value on the words. Most people recognized another way to communicate, and that is through the heart and through the silence. Even if Almira's words were what the people wanted to hear, they could also hear the silence radiating from her. Why? Because that's where she lived her life.

"So much is overlooked in the world we live in," Almira began. "In our haste, we forget to see the real experience of life. We forget to live it.

"With baby-like steps, we start the journey of re-discovery. Rediscovering the joy of the hugeness of who we are and the important part every single person plays. There is not one person that should be living a life of pain. In fact every person's role is vital for the expansion of consciousness. Consciousness has to evolve and expand and that is the role of the human. That is what we are here to do. Sometimes we get caught thinking it's about our job or relationship, when in fact what the human is doing is healing the consciousness that holds all life in order.

"There are no accidents or mistakes. From a condemning or negative view, we could see a lot of imperfection. But in reality all are playing out their roles to help everyone rediscover their birthright. What is really going on is amazing in its interwovenness. There is a divine harmony and order to all. The role of the human is to discover that and to live that harmony. From that place we are doing the greatest service to mankind, to the planet and to the universe, that we could imagine. The role of the teacher is to ignite the flame lying dormant inside of us, so we can see that the passion exists.

"To begin with, we feel like we are doing it for ourselves, so we can experience a better life, more happiness, better health, more peace. But as our experience grows and the experience of life changes we realize we are doing it for everyone else also. In fact, there is no greater service than to hold the hand out, with all the wisdom, and invite someone else to better his or her life. There comes a time when nothing else compares to that, and in fact anything less is a waste of time.

"The huge expansion and joy experienced when someone else's face lights up in knowledge that they are wonderful, powerful, beautiful expressions of the divine, is worth everything. It's the pure joy of giving it away. It is pure compassion.

"Pure compassion has nothing to do with what most people think the word compassion means. It is not apathy. It is not pity. True compassion is the marriage of the unconditional love of the universe with the wisdom of the universe. Said another way, true compassion is to offer somebody the truth while meeting them where they are at. Instead of agreeing with the drama, the fear or the problems, you have a greater understanding of life and share that. So you are not pulled down into the lower energies that most of the people experience and share. Instead you stand firm and unwavering in the universal truth and gently guide others to that. By far, the greatest compassion is one we mostly forget about, and that is true compassion for ourselves.

"You deserve to be free. You deserve to live a wondrous life. True compassion in its greatest sense is recognizing the negativity we create within our mind, that we then believe to be real, and the misery we choose to inflict upon ourselves. We are the greatest source of our misery. We are! When we make the choice to let those self-violent, self defeating thoughts go, then we are engaged in the greatest act of compassion to the universe. Ironically, that is the greatest act of surrender and also the greatest act of power. It is your power. It is your power of choice and by choosing for the experience of the divinity within, you are giving up the little limited self to the greatness of the universe to give you everything.

"Unconditional love is the absolute essence of who you really are. True compassion is the movement of that love out into creation.

"Most people spend most of their lives attached to their mind. They are guided by thousands of thoughts that run through their mind and run their existence. They are bound to those thoughts and so are sentenced to the tug-of-war of the conflicts those thoughts impose. The thoughts of indecisiveness, the negativity, the fear, the judgments, are running in your mind, and you believe them to be real.

"They are not you, they are not real. When people hear these words, it might seem too far beyond them or too mystical. But the true teaching is in the experience.

"When people are guided by the simplest techniques to recognize, in their own experience, that they are not those thoughts, that in itself is life changing.

"Maybe for the first time they recognize the power of the silence. Maybe for the first time they experience deep peace. Maybe for the first time they recognize they have the power of choice to let all that conflict from the mind go. And with a little practice it can be gone permanently. Isn't that amazing! And that is just the beginning. Recognizing that you are not those thoughts is just the start of this amazing adventure.

"We have been bound to the mind and so we learn to let go of that bondage and to experience something else. From that place the world is a playground. Life is an adventure of exploration and peace. Can you imagine living life constantly in peace and joy and playing in the divinity of all things? Can you imagine experiencing eternity in every moment and knowing without a doubt the perfection of existence? Can you imagine having so much love for yourself and your life that all you see and all you experience is that love? It sounds too good to be true, doesn't it? That is a common comment from people I talk to.

"The greatest realization is knowing nothing you have done in your life has been wrong. It has all been perfect to make you want a greater experience of life. And now that desire that you have has been answered by the universe. It's no accident you are listening to my words. It's no accident you are here. The choice for you now is whether you act on it or not. Are you willing to take the next step? Once you know you have the ability to make a difference in your life, the next step is doing it.

"That is why I am here. That is why the teaching of the Ishayas' Ascension exists. You cannot do this on your own. Some very few people have. They have woken up into full human consciousness, full enlightenment, and their life was forever changed. They might write books, or they might have students, but it's very rare for them to actually lead someone else into their own experience of oneness. Why? Because this path of waking up needs guidance from someone who has done it.

"We teach a series of very simple techniques that are mechanical. They are not a belief or a religion. They are mechanical techniques that satisfy the left and right hemispheres of the brain bringing about automatic coherence in the brain waves. This coherence in the brain is the scientific way of describing the expansion you experience in consciousness. It's a removal of the constant barrage of the ninety thousand thoughts we think a day. It is so simple and effortless. The techniques can be used with the eyes closed in meditation or with the eyes open as you go about your daily life. They instantly create the harmony of body and brain and bring you fully into the present moment. It's only in the present moment that you can experience the wonder of the universe, the freshness of life. A natural byproduct is the amazing rest the body receives and with that rest amazing levels of healing or regeneration can take place naturally. This teaching is phenomenal in its simplicity and its directness. It's phenomenal in what I see happen to people within a weekend course, and a few weeks and months later. The world becomes your playground. I am honored to be a teacher of this incredible teaching and to be in service to others who want to know more. It is so easy.

"But it comes back to you. The choice is yours. Now that you have listened to what I have had to say, now that you have felt your heart enliven, now that you have related your own experiences to these, what are you going to do? Are you willing to make a step in the direction of a greater life for yourself? One that gives you more than your wildest dreams?

"Knowing that you have a choice is the first step to making the choice. So, the choice is up to you."

Life doesn't have to be hard.
You may have hiccups and you might forget for a bit.
But thinking is the only thing that can cause you pain.
It's the only thing that can cause you anguish.
But you have to continue to be ruthless with your desire to wake up.
This is your life.
This is the beginning.

What is an Ishaya?

I was sitting in front of a large class. Over the past twenty-four hours, the participants had been introduced to two of the four techniques being taught over the weekend. This is what happens: on Friday night they begin, coming to class with their concerns, their stresses and even their skepticisms. But in them is always the force that drove them there. And that force is the desire to change their life somehow. Three hours later we send them home to practice the first technique, and it's common to see them leave that night full of questions. On Saturday I always watch a transformation taking place right in front of my eyes. The doors are opening wider in their consciousness. The walls surrounding their hearts are melting. Always by the afternoon the light is burning bright in their eyes and people are radiating a peace that wasn't there less than twenty-four hours before. That is the stunning speed with which someone's life can change. It's the speed of these techniques. And I see it so often.

My heart just keeps swelling with love for these beautiful people. I always see them as the Divine Source they truly are, but they just don't know it. I see the light return to their hearts and their eyes. It's a humbling knowledge, the greatness of consciousness, itself, which is making the change.

The more I teach, the more I sit in front of classes, I know it is not about me. People feel the power of the Divine whether I speak or not. They experience it solely in my presence, because that is what I'm experiencing. And that alone, will raise their consciousness. The words and conversations played out throughout the weekend are simply another way of conveying that same information. One passes it on, in all its strength and power, in the silence. The other passes it on through words, examples, drawings and conceptualizations of what the silence is.

It is so expanding for me to share with people what consciousness is. I'm sharing my heart, my passion for humanity to wake up, and also sharing that they have the power to make that experience be their own. It is up to them. Maybe for the first time in their lives they see they hold the power of choice. Not from a stubborn, aggressive place, but from the simple desire to love themselves.

The power and transformation from that desire is life changing. There have been beautiful studies done on the effects of consciousness on the human body and on the planet. It's astounding what is truly going on when we make that choice. At first we feel like we are doing it for ourselves as we desire a better, happier life for ourselves. But the impact of making that choice affects the planet to a staggering degree. The power of positive thinking has now been recorded in books and on websites by different meditation groups and scientists for everyone to see for themselves.

One little book I adore is *Messages from Water*. The author has been photographing ice crystals for years. His book shows photos of ice crystals formed after the words "I hate you" were said to water, compared to crystals formed after the words "I love you" were said. It also shows crystals formed by the water when it was ignored. The many different examples show that water has a consciousness and we have the ability to create a beautiful world through love and harmony or to destroy ourselves and the planet through hate.

Most of the people who come to us recognize they are destroying themselves. They are getting sick, emotional, tired, and unhappy. They recognize they want to change that. By the end of the weekend, just forty-eight hours, the common experience of the class is one of union and joy. Faces are showing a depth of peace that wasn't there earlier. Eyes shine with a radiance of worthiness, and love and appreciation are voiced.

It is so humbling to receive this praise, as it's how they should be experiencing life. They simply forgot and needed guiding in the right direction.

The teachers of the Bright Path are people who have recognized the one truth on the planet. And that one truth is freedom. Freedom from the negativity, the reactive patterns and the suffering. Anything else falls short of the experience of the peace of living your life from the presence of the Ascendant, the presence of God. An Ishaya is someone who has dedicated their life to knowing and living that truth for themselves, and then giving that knowledge to the rest of humanity. They have recognized the truth and are constantly living life from that higher consciousness. Anything less would be a lie. We teach that it is real, so what could a teacher who isn't experiencing that possibly teach? It would be a pretty hollow teaching, based on concepts and assumptions. We have no need to teach that way, as we experience the truth all the time. And so it is we share with people who have the hearts to listen.

In my experience, people know in themselves a true teaching where a teacher is living the teaching, or a false teaching in which the teacher isn't. There is a huge difference between the two. The first teaching is grounded in absolute unwavering truth as the teacher is experiencing it. The answer to a question doesn't come from a textbook, but rather from the teacher's direct experience as they moved into the higher states of consciousness. That is vital for the students' growth. It is unwavering truth, not distorted by assumptions or perception. Any other teaching can only be based in assumptions. And that is as useful as trying to describe what a rambutan tastes like if someone has never tasted one. The description is worthless compared to the person trying the fruit, and so is the teaching.

We teach that the higher states of consciousness are your birthright, and as an Ishaya teacher we must be having a constant awareness of the higher states. Anything less than that is unworthy of being called a teacher. The focus we have when we sit in front of the class is the same focus as when we are driving in a car or watching a movie. It is perpetual, natural and easy; but it has to be perpetual.

Once again, it's not about us as individuals, but as living representations that the universal energy can be permanently acknowledged and maintained in the world. That everyone can have that experience. The common belief is that you have to remove yourself from this world to experience that unbounded peace. Does that mean people who have families and careers have to give them up? Does that mean the joy of the universe is not in the children or in the career? Many people don't pursue a spiritual path, or they stop along the path, in fear of having to give up what is theirs. This world, this life, you, are that source of everything. There is no place where the source is not. Everyone, no matter what his or her life path, has the ability to be living it in the joy and bliss the universe has to offer. There are no exceptions.

There is no one way it looks. There are no rules. There is only the need or the desire for more, and instantly the universe responds. The universe wants you to have it all. We have been the idiots that have been creating a hard life for ourselves. We might then try to blame others, but it always comes back to us. Living in peace in this busy world might seem like a fairy tale or hard work, but it always comes back to the same thing. That you have a choice. The busy world then becomes the teacher to propel you into the higher states of consciousness. It becomes the playground to play in. Every moment and every situation gives you the opportunity to live in fear, hate and reactions, or to love and be grateful.

It's not the forcing of a mind-created concept, like, "I have to be loving. I have to be loving!" That is what affirmations are. Sometimes they work, and sometimes they don't. It's a lot easier to have the direct experience of gratitude and love built into your life, so that is what you naturally choose when you see a choice needs to be made.

An Ishaya is somebody who transmits that knowledge to all of humanity regardless of who, what, where, when or how. All that is needed is the desire for more.

Everyone in this world is looking for the same thing. Everyone is looking for the meaning in his or her life and to experience love. The love that's dreamed about. The love that's sung about. Not the love in movies of heartbreak and adventure, but the sense of completeness that seems so rare, so hard to find.

People come to Ascension for the same thing. When asked, they might not even know that is what their heart is yearning for. But all desires are based on the same thing.

It takes a special type of person to be able to guide others to that. The only way to be able to do it is to have the direct experience of that unconditional love themselves. That, combined with the life experiences of pain and separation before experiencing the unconditional love, makes a teacher able to meet people where they are at, and to show them another choice. That is the structure of true compassion.

The four techniques we teach on the weekend are based around praise, gratitude, love and compassion, four emotions or qualities having the power to transform lives. Out of the four techniques we teach, unconditional love and true compassion are the two emotions, or states of being, that just aren't understood. People don't experience them, so they don't understand them. As teachers of the truth, we teach from the place of constant unconditional love and constant true compassion.

Love is the force that holds all people and things together in harmony. It's unconditional, without judgment and forever. Compassion is the natural movement of that force. It's the power behind the words, the energy in people's eyes.

Compassion is very interesting, and often misunderstood. Sometimes, the greatest compassion could be to destroy somebody's ignorance to make them realize the experience of the Ascendant is greater. But always it is the formula of unconditional love plus wisdom. Even those words in the formula, however, can become merely concepts. The greatest teacher is the experience itself.

For me, the experience of compassion has evolved as my experience of the universe has evolved. My experience of loving unconditionally has deepened and become more and more real, as my experience of the Ascendant has deepened.

This world needs love and compassion so badly. Healing humanity is actually a part of the vows we take. What are we healing humanity from? From the belief and the pain of feeling separate from each other and from God, and from the illusion that we are not the true creators of our lives, that is, the belief that we are victims. Ninety-nine percent of the world walks around in this state, and the only way to heal that is through love. It is the only way. It is the only experience. God is that love. The universe is that love. We are that love. Compassion is the power and movement of that love.

You cannot force someone to want to make the choice. You cannot hit them over the head with conscious concepts and make them wake up. You then have become a piece of the negative energy. You have added to the angry, negative energy already destroying the consciousness on this planet. You have become part of the problem.

The only way is the way of the truth. The way of living the experience of compassion and unconditional love. In that way people hold the power to make the choice for themselves. The teacher simply represents the highest choice in the universe. The choice for living the experience of freedom. People recognize that freedom in their hearts, and their hearts yearn for it. That is then the power of transformation. That is then the power of choice.

"Think of your most perfect moment.
Do you remember how perfectly it unfolded, miraculously?
There was nothing about the moment you would change. It was ideal.
We weren't responsible for that moment, it just happened.
It was the most alive moment of your life!
You are meant to live that kind of life, be that alive.
That is your Right, to live that kind of life.
But we don't.
We just forgot."

M.K.I.

——————— ———————

My experience

by Jaya Ishaya

I have always known the absolute joy that being in nature brings me. As a child I used to walk for hours on our farm, deep in the adventures of a young imagination. I would sing and laugh to myself. I would create worlds in dreams and fantasies. Life was magical. Often my brother and sister would be with me and we would all be ecstatic in the joy of playing in life. As I grew older, I always carried that connection to nature with me. Even in the craziest moments of my life, I always knew to go for a walk on the beach, or to sit in my garden to bring about an inner peace and an inner smile within me. I never forgot that connection.

Many times, I was aware of the intense contrast between the two experiences. First there was the experience of being in the world and getting frustrated, angry, or disillusioned, which was very painful for me. Then there was the experience of joy, beauty and connectedness that I experienced when I simply was still and in appreciation for the world and for my life. It was incredible I didn't focus on the second experience more. I was so aware of it, but the direction my life headed was toward total forgetfulness of what the child had known to exist. The challenges became more intense. The comparisons and the judgments became more real.

Soon, I lost track of the 'connectedness' and came to believe what I needed was simply the sitting in the garden or the walking on the beach. In short, the adult had forgotten the real magic that exists.

My life was the life that most people experienced. My happiness depended on how my friends treated me. And if I was stubborn enough to do things on my own, then I was lonely. It was a roller coaster. And I was on the roller coaster for years. I thought it was normal, as everyone else complained, laughed, complained and laughed also. But everyone was searching. What for? For more of life. For the happiness. For their real purpose. Very few seemed to find it.

And I was searching too. I just didn't think about it. I kind of drifted into partying, and into meaningless jobs. Most people experience this. And most people experience moments of peace, however fleeting or long. But most people, however, have no idea that experience can and should be permanent. I know I didn't. I loved the sunsets over the ocean. I often went to watch those ten or fifteen minutes of nature's gift to me. I would experience the awe, the peace and the love. But in reality, I didn't put value on those moments. I didn't understand that peace. I knew and loved the experience, but then I had to return to my life. As soon as I turned away from what I was witnessing, I was thinking about something else again and the connection was lost.

I couldn't live my life watching sunsets continuously, so I never dreamt that feeling of awe and experience of oneness could be more than those fleeting moments.

Everyone has moments of peace. That is what has been shown in this book. From different walks of life and different scenarios with different people, there is a common thread, the same underlying desire to experience great peace. The stories show how easy it is to experience it. The most confusing thing for most people is once they have experienced it, they don't know how to experience it again.

That is where the Ishayas of The Bright Path changed my life. I learnt the techniques, which were so simple and easy. At that time I still had the ignorance and arrogance that nothing needed to change in my life, although I constantly wanted it to. So I didn't use the techniques with my eyes closed in meditation much at all. I did use them with my eyes open all the time, and I was very aware of the instantaneous changes in my perception and in my appreciation for seeing life in the present moment. These techniques can be used with the eyes open anywhere, and for me the changes were obvious.

Surprisingly, I didn't acknowledge the subtle changes in me until a major change in my life took place. But in the absolute perfection of it all, I saw I couldn't look outside of myself for my happiness: everything I had invested my security and purpose in had the potential to change. I wasn't going to shut out my world, but rather, I experienced the intense peace, strength, and inner power of the present moment, in *me*.

In those vital moments, I saw with intense clarity what I experience and teach today. I saw the choice. That it was up to me to change my reality. I could focus on the problems, the drama and the negativity, which could lead me to depression and pain, or I could focus on the positive and discover the beauty that was still constantly in my life.

As the days and weeks passed, I saw that choice over and over again. The choice was mine and I decided to choose for my peace. It was the most incredible experience, as I had never before known how powerful I was.

The choice was carved into stone. One door had closed and another had opened for me. In a matter of months I had put myself on an airplane aimed at living my life fully and fulfilling what I wanted to do, for me. I had no idea what that meant, but I was letting everything go.

I was guided with incredible precision, without hesitation, to the Ishayas. In my mind, I was visiting for a few weeks to learn a few techniques, and then I was going to travel around the world and visit all these cool energy places, like Peru and India.

I had no idea what I was walking into. I arrived at a large house that was hosting the retreat center. I walked in all bouncy and filled with nervous energy. I walked into silence. The house was in total silence. There were maybe ten people in the living room, all with their eyes closed. An hour later was dinner time, and they had their eyes open but they still didn't talk much. Nobody cared for the random rattle that was flowing out of my mouth.

That evening we all met in the living room again. This time there were maybe twenty people. As we introduced ourselves we had to say why we were here. I hated crowds and talking in them, so I was very nervous when the person beside me started talking, as I knew my turn was next.

I said my name, and then I experienced someone speaking that wasn't me, who said I was here for enlightenment. I stared at the teacher for a long moment. Our eyes were locked. Time became normal again, and I had no idea why I had just said that. I barely knew what the word meant. I felt embarrassed. I was in a room full of reiki masters and people who had been meditating for many years. I felt so silly and unknowledgeable.

After the introductions the two main teachers began to talk. All my insecurities started melting. The words they were saying were astounding my mind and opening my heart. I knew in that meeting that I could not leave. After the next couple of meetings, I knew that I couldn't leave ever. It felt like the most radical, spontaneous thing to do, but the most normal and unquestionable. My heart had recognized the truth. My heart had recognized home. I had recognized my true purpose for being on this planet.

It was then that I knew that I was, without a doubt, a monk of the ancient tradition of The Bright Path. I knew that I was doing it again, as I had done many times before in other lives.

It was like putting on a familiar jacket. There was no hesitation or question. It was natural and complete trust in the universe. But beyond that, I knew I was walking towards freedom. I had complete trust these people in front of me could and would give that to me.

Previously I lived to buy shoes, makeup and party, and then almost overnight I had stopped. The funny thing was, I really had no idea what I was doing. I was in fact doing nothing! I was for the first time in my life letting go of all the expectations I had of myself, all the numerous beliefs, and in doing that I was experiencing a joy for life that was beyond words. I was experiencing a love for myself I had never experienced. I was experiencing a genuine, constant and pure love for everyone else and for all things. In fact the love I was discovering was so real that everything I had experienced previously in my life paled in comparison.

The fact I hadn't done anything else spiritual wasn't a problem. In fact, because of my innocence and willingness I experienced huge transformations quickly. Those transformations have continued to occur as my experience and dedication to the silence have changed. The experience becomes so stable that the idea of the emotional roller coaster is very contrasting. There is absolutely no reason to experience fear and negativity ever again. The simplicity of it all is stunning.

I totally thank all the Ishayas for who I am, what I know and the amazing life I live, which is being in service to give constantly in any way I can to help the world, and me, to wake up.

As I write this now, I have been an Ishaya monk for a number of years. I have had the honour of teaching hundreds of wonderful people the joys of meditation and the beauty of living a fuller life. I have watched the consciousness of the planet shift and change. The thing that never ceases to amaze me is just how fast someone's life can transform. We constantly watch people come to us at the beginning of a course with faces filled with fear, doubt and concerns. Two days later they are transformed into light and laughter. Sometimes the radical changes happen in just one day. They never have to return to living in fear and chaos. Once they have been made aware of it, it's then just a simple choice. With the tools to help make the choice and with the guidance from someone who has done it, dramatic changes in people's consciousness will happen.

We constantly hear stories from people who have had amazing health breakthroughs. And we constantly see the results for ourselves. That is because almost all (if not all) illnesses are created in the mind. Every thought we think has a direct response in the trillions of cells in our bodies. We think negatively; we create negativity, tension, stress and illness in our bodies. We think positively, and harmony is instantaneously experienced between all those cells. Even greater than the positive thoughts is the silence of not thinking. All thoughts are created from that space and are neither positive nor negative. The greatest healings and transformations take place from the silence. The cells are in continuous communication with each other. The human body is an amazing make up of intelligence. Yet we feed it negativity, and it deteriorates. Love holds the highest vibration, and every cell in your body hums to the highest vibration when we are thinking or experiencing love. The silence is the greatest expression of pure unconditional love.

I had the idea that to experience the silence meant that you had to be in an environment that was still and silent. How could that be possible in a world filled with noise and movement? Paradoxically, as you start to experience the silence within, you start to experience the silence amidst all the noise and the movement in the world. And then you realize it has always been there, in its wonder and glory. We just failed to see and experience it.

Suddenly the responsibility has been put back into our hands. We are not the victims of some outside influence. Instead, we are the powerful creators with the choice. How incredible!

Often on the Saturday of the course, not even twenty-four hours into the class, students look radiant, more relaxed, and brighter. Maybe they have had a full night's sleep for the first time in years. Maybe they have noticed they are no longer experiencing anxiety.

Sometimes we go back into a community after a few months and people who were on twenty medications for various disorders, are down to three, as their health and well being have improved so dramatically.

The most phenomenal, ongoing learning I see in others and in myself is the dance of the mind. It's the "waking up" to seeing what the mind really is, and that it's just thoughts that will go by, if we let them. But those thoughts are what we have listened to, believed, and succumbed to over and over again for years. We have then personalized these thoughts and called them the ego. We have created them, structured them and believed in this individual personality so strongly, that even if it brings us pain, we still recreate it over and over.

It is absolutely astounding to see this clearly, and then to have the guidance and the tools to break the habit of identifying with these thoughts. It's absolutely stunning to watch other people realize for the first time in their life that those thoughts go by, and they have the choice to put attention on them and believe them to be real, or not! By making the choice not to, the most amazing experience of life starts to unfold. One that is without stress and fear. One that is filled with awe and wonder. One that is filled with a gentle, pure, unconditional love for oneself and for all. It is an incomparable experience, so easily obtained, it leaves you wondering, *why?* Why did we bother to be so violent, destructive and self-condemning for so long?

The answer to that is so you could have the experience of immense gratitude for realizing there is a choice.

For my Teacher.